point is that the critical inquiry of the university (and its dissemination thereof) stands in dialectical opposition both to mere dogma and to the insecurity of mere consensual relativism. Our problem then is to discover a foundation upon which we might with appropriate security regard the intellectual role of the university. The under-girding I propose consists in the university's enactment of temporality. Therein lies its fundamental task and its justification.

IV

As will be made clear in this section, criticisms of my model of the university may be derived either from the left, center, or right regions of the socio-political continuum.

To begin in the center of the continuum, Clark Kerr adopts an *historicist* position which argues that the university ought to reduce its role to that of meeting the strictly contemporary demands of technology. In a speech titled "The Idea of the Multiversity" delivered at Harvard University in 1963, Kerr makes his position obvious. That speech along with other of Kerr's meditations on the university was published in *The Uses of the University*.[1] Not seeking to hide his historicism Kerr writes: "What is the justification of the modern American multiversity? History is one answer. Consistency with the surrounding society is another."[2] As if that were not clear enough he later writes: "The process cannot be stopped. The results cannot be foreseen. It remains to adapt."[3] Now it is evident from these passages that in Kerr's view the role of the university demands – at least in the United States – adaptation to the society which surrounds it.[4] But since the apparent source of the obligation to make this adaptation is history, it is not certain whether Kerr means to say that the

[1] Clark Kerr, *The Uses of the University* (New York: Harper & Row, 1966.)

[2] Kerr, pp. 44–45.

[3] Kerr, p. 124.

[4] It is further evident that the logic of Kerr's argument – though he does not extend it this far – commits him to saying that whatever society a university is in it must adapt to it. If Kerr does not give assent to this more general thesis, then it is not clear why universities ought to adapt to this society. And if Kerr does assent to the general thesis, then it is clear that he is wrong.

Tulane Studies in Philosophy

VOLUME XXII

Dewey and his Influence

ESSAYS IN HONOR
OF GEORGE ESTES BARTON

edited by

ROBERT C. WHITTEMORE

TULANE UNIVERSITY

NEW ORLEANS

1973

ISBN 90 247 1565 2

316277

PRINTED IN THE NETHERLANDS

CONTENTS

PREFACE

To those of us who have been privileged to call him colleague, Georges Estes Barton is perhaps best and most fondly remembered as the man with a camera. At the beginning of every semester he could be observed carefully photographing each of his arriving students, and while we used to chaff him about this practice, all of us respected the motive behind it. For George Barton was and is a dedicated teacher and in his courses no student ever would be suffered to remain simply a face in the crowd.

His favorite teaching technique has always been Socratic discourse, and he is, as Professors Roberts and DuBose remind us in their essays for this volume, a master of the method. In his chosen field of philosophy of education he has long been recognized as a leader, serving several terms on the Executive Committee of the Philosophy of Education Society and in 1963 as its President. In 1966 St. Edwards University conferred upon him the honorary degree LL.D in recognition of his significant contributions to curriculum development.

Following a distinguished career in general education and educational research at the Rochester Institute of Technology and at the University of Chicago, Professor Barton was appointed in 1956 to direct Tulane's Inter-Disciplinary Program for the Preparation of Liberally Educated Teachers. In February 1962, having seen the program through to a successful conclusion, he joined the Department of Philosophy at Newcomb College as Associate Professor of Philosophy. The year following he was named Visiting Scholar in the Center for the Study of Liberal Education for Adults, Fund for Adult Education, at the University of Chicago, and upon his return to Tulane in the autumn of 1963 he was promoted

Professor of Philosophy in Newcomb College. From 1966 through 1969 he served as Head of the Newcomb Department. He retired from active teaching in June 1971.

Throughout his academic life Professor Barton's prime philosophical interest has been in the philosophy, particularly the educational philosophy, of John Dewey. He has regularly taught the seminar in Dewey, and the several contributions in the present volume devoted to various aspects of Dewey's thought reflect the influence of his teaching. With much appreciation, then, and with deep affection, we commend these essays to his discretion.

ROBERT C. WHITTEMORE
New Orleans, Louisiana

THE VERY IDEA OF A UNIVERSITY

HAROLD ALDERMAN
California State College, Sonoma

I

In 1852 John Henry Cardinal Newman gave a series of nine lectures which was designed to justify the establishing of the University of Dublin as a Catholic University. The title of that series of lectures was, of course, *The Idea of a University*[1] and it was Newman's goal to describe the unique, essential role of the university and then to demonstrate the place of the university within a Catholic society. In my view Newman's division of his problem into these two aspects yields a paradigm for anyone who would discuss the contemporary university. For this reason I have chosen to title this philosophical sketch of the university with a variation on Newman's title.

But it is the variation that makes the relation between our titles interesting. For with the addition of the word 'very' I both emphasize the defining properties of a university and call attention to the differences between the problems faced by Newman and the problems faced by anyone who would today attempt to define and justify the university. In the first place, Newman's work consists of an argument for a university which was to be founded; to write about the university today, however, requires that one defend an established institution which is undergoing various dangerous – if not serious – ideological attacks. Thus whereas for Newman the idea of a university was questioned, today the very idea of a university has become questionable: thereby the main difference in our titles. For Newman the problem was to define a university for those who were not sure what one was. The task of the contemporary writer is to re-define and to defend the idea of a university at a time when everyone claims with equal con-

---

[1] John Henry Cardinal Newman, *The Idea of a University* (London: Longmans, Green and Company, 1911).

fidence both to know what a university is and also to know that whatever it is, it is not very important.

Succinctly, it is the thesis of this paper that: *The unique role of the university is to enact a care for human temporality. In the dual functions of teaching and scholarship, the past and the future are made present.* In order to elaborate and defend this thesis I shall in section II briefly describe the activity of the medieval university and shall interpret this activity in terms of Martin Heidegger's description of temporality. In section III I shall develop a criticism of Newman's magisterial work. In section IV I shall describe and reject several contemporary conceptions of the university which deny its essentially historical character. Section V is a summary and an exhortation.

II

However important the contributions of Athens to the development of the western concern with theory, it is clear that universities, as institutions wherein that concern is made explicit, are strictly a contribution of the late middle ages.[1] Prior to the foundation of the Universities of Bologna and Paris in the 12th century, there were of course monastic schools which were concerned with "higher learning." But according to Charles Homer Haskins, the introduction of "new knowledge" from the Greeks, the Arabs, and the Romans resulted in a secularization of learning that gave birth to the universities.[2] This "secularization" displaced the traditional trivium of grammar, rhetoric and logic and the advanced quadrivium of arithmetic, geometry, astronomy and music, and emphasized in their place "the works of Aristotle, Euclid, Ptolemy, and the Greek physicians, the new arithmetic, and those texts of the Roman law which had lain hidden through the dark ages."[3] With the introduction of these subjects social

---

[1] Charles Homer Haskins, *The Rise of Universities* (Ithaca: Cornell University Press, 1970), p. 1.

[2] Haskins, pp. 4–5.

[3] Haskins, p. 5.

demands were created for institutions in which men could be educated into the professions of law and medicine.

Now it seems to me that what is crucial in this historical development is not simply the secularization of learning; rather it is the introduction of *new* learning. The *teaching* activities of the monasteries necessarily had to be supplemented in order to assimilate and cope with the newly discovered ideas. With this additional, complex task the universities became distinguishable from the monastic schools not only in that they had to *pass on* new information, but more importantly in that they had to *appropriate* it.

The monastic schools, then, existed as institutions to pass along a tradition; the universities as a response to the twelfth century renaissance not only passed along the tradition but interpreted, applied, and expanded it. The new universities were *historical* because in addition to their complex, interpretative concern with the past, they applied learning to the present through the development of the professions and anticipated the future through the theoretical elaboration of the new ideas.

But if there was one over-riding pre-occupation of the medieval university, it was *teaching*. Students, whether at Paris or Bologna, were an important focal point in the retrieval of the Greek, Latin and Arab texts whose introduction into Europe gave impetus to the foundation of the university. Thus the faculty of the medieval university were scholar-teachers involved in the dual role of discovery and dissemination. But the students themselves were *students* because they entered into an active role in that dissemination. Together teachers and students defined the university as an institution dedicated to "the consecration of learning."[1] Thus an essential element in the medieval model of the university was the activity of teaching through which professors insured the survival of the important, tripartite concern for time.

Concern for each of the moments of time and concern for the dissemination of that concern are then the distinguishing characteristics of the university in its very earliest days. Of course, the *fact* that these concerns did characterize the uni-

[1] Haskins, p. 25.

versity is no argument that they ought to. In order to make the normative argument it is also necessary to show that being temporal is a fundamental feature of being human.

It seems to me that the most forceful reminder of the temporal character of being human is found in the work of Martin Heidegger. It is his phenomenological description of human temporality which supports my model of the university. Briefly, in Heidegger's view western thinkers have for the most part treated time as if it were some objective and neutral measuring device.[1] By approaching time in this fashion it has been reified and detached from its originary locus within human experience. Because of this detachment a fundamental feature of time – or better of *temporality* – has been overlooked: man is the time-keeping being. Time in Heidegger's analysis is thus a human *activity* of ordering experience.

There are in Heidegger's view two possibilities of human temporality. The first of these he terms owned (*eigentlich*) temporality and it is characterized as an explicitly worldly mode of keeping time in which each of the moments of time (past, present and future) are *significantly* open. In this mode of being temporal, man fully appropriates his temporality as a project of his own making; he understands that having a history, being temporal, means to significantly order one's experience of events. Human time-keeping becomes an ordering of experience in terms of the ultimately past moment (birth) and the ultimately future moment (death). Through the activity of remaining open to these most significant of all moments, man learns to accept his fate as a being who projects himself in a present moment, from a past moment to a future moment. Man *makes* history.

On the other hand, disowned (*uneigentlich*) time exemplifies man's objective treatment of time as a container in which moments are only related in terms of before and after. In this mode of appropriation man is not responsible for *his* time because he appears to be not making time but only watching it pass. In addition to the eschewal of responsibility, dis-owned temporality results in the fragmentation of time's essential

---

[1] See my paper "Heidegger on Being Human," *Philosophy Today*, vol. 15, no. 4, Spring 1971 for an elaboration of the following statement.

unity. With these two developments, existence in the mode of dis-owned time amounts to a denial of man's temporal being: it becomes a form of ignorance.

In summary, in its very earliest days the university manifested a regard for man's temporal nature through its concern for the past, present, and future and through disseminating that concern in teaching. Heidegger's description of temporality provides a matrix within which this concern is made intelligible as a mode of enacting (i.e., evincing care for) human temporality. The tripartite concern of the medieval university thus provides a paradigm of what the university ought to be. It is in the light of this paradigm that I shall in the next two sections criticize first Newman's and then three contemporary statements which represent denials of the university's essential concern with human temporality.

III

Newman opens his argument by asserting that universities are concerned *only* with teaching. He writes that the university is

a place of *teaching* universal *knowledge*. This implies that its object is, on the one hand, intellectual, not moral; and, on the other, that it is the diffusion and extension of knowledge rather than the advancement.[1]

In this passage Newman suggests a number of points important to developing my model of the university. In the first place, his separation of teaching and scholarship is based on the practical grounds that it is simpler to do both if you divide the two activities and assign them to different institutions. This may indeed be true; but my argument against such a separation is that teaching becomes decadent when it is disassociated from scholarship and that scholarship becomes blind (mere research) when separated from the tradition which is continually re-encountered in teaching. Both this decadence and this blindness are forms of temporal disruption. In effect, to isolate the teaching function from scholarship is to present the student with a teacher who has himself ceased to actively

[1] Newman, p. IX.

engage temporality. He who only teaches thus does not exemplify the concern he disseminates. On the other hand the mere *researcher* is unable to situate his work within a tradition by anticipating a future in which that work will be cared for.

A number of positive suggestions, however, are also made by Newman in the above passage. The most important of these is that the goal of the university is intellectual rather than moral instruction. With this point, Newman of course was more interested in defending the church than in defending the university, but this does not restrict usage of Newman's defense to his own usage. Also, Newman suggests that the university is concerned not merely with intellectual knowledge but with universal knowledge. If by universal knowledge we also include knowledge of those general principles which govern the specialized professions of, for example, law and medicine, then I have no objection. But it is clear that Newman means by 'universal knowledge' that knowledge gained in the liberal arts and sciences. In his view the university exclusively pursued such liberal education as an end in itself.[1] With this position Newman both establishes his reputation as the prototypical intellectualist and also opens his argument to the charge of being atemporal in that it allows no central role for the present moment in the university's life.

Despite the problems I have suggested in Newman's idea of the university, his book is a thesaurus for anyone concerned about the intellectual role of that institution. But Newman's confidence in that intellectual role is founded on his faith in the absolute truth of the Christian revelation. Thus it was his assumption that the truths disseminated in the university would not conflict with the truths of revealed religion; or he believed that if there was such conflict, it was due quite simply to a mistake or to an improper encroachment of secular knowledge upon the domain of theology.

Without some such grounding – and it is clear that we cannot simply adopt the theological one accepted by Newman – the role of the university becomes very questionable. The

[1] Newman, p. 177.

university will adapt or ought to adapt. Indeed, the point of his historicism is to remove the distinction between fact and value. The multiversity is what it is not because men enacting their own projects created it but because the objective forces of history produced it.[1]

Kerr's position thus represents a disruption of temporal continuity by treating the present moment (i.e., contemporary society) as if it were isolated from past and future. Because of the fragmentation of time which underlies Kerr's idea of the multiversity, that institution is itself fragmented. It is not one community but rather a mere association of many. In this regard the multiversity appropriately reflects the surrounding society. Further, within the multiversity the dominant community to which reasonable men apparently ought to give obeisance is the atemporal research institute which, disassociated from teaching, represents the dominant element of contemporary society – business technology. Again one notes the harmonious consonance of all the elements of Kerr's position: not only does the dominant community within the multiversity reflect the interests of the dominant element in society, but the activity with which researchers are involved – technology – is itself atemporal.[2] Everything fits; except that we have forgotten the past and the future. This forgetfulness is of course the perfect expression of Kerr's strict contemporaneity.[3]

But strict contemporaneity is not the prerogative of the center. It exists in a number of forms on what I suppose is the social-political-academic left. The two main versions of this contemporaneity have been described by Robert Nisbet as "The Deluge of Humanitarianism" and "The Cult of Individuality."[4] In the first case the argument is that the university's

---

[1] Kerr, p. 9.

[2] For an elaboration of this point see my paper "Heidegger: Technology as Phenomenon," *Personalist*, vol. 51 #4, Autumn, 1970.

[3] At the very end of his book Kerr apparently realizes what he has gotten himself into. He writes: "The intellect, and the university as its most happy home, can have great potential roles to play in the reconciliation of the war between the future and the past...." p. 126.
Given Kerr's argument however this passage is simply a quixotic non-sequitur and the reconciliation, given his view, can hardly even be said to be *potential*.

[4] Robert Nisbet, *The Degradation of the Academic Dogma* (New York: Basic Books, 1971) Chapters 8 and 9.

raison d'être is social engineering designed to insure the welfare of disadvantaged minorities. But this is obviously only the social-worker-technician's analog of the business technicians' idea of the university. Both of them manifest a barbarism which denies the structured relation of past and future to the present. Because it is this parallel lack of temporal awareness that is pertinent to my argument, I need not pursue discussion of this first position. I mention it only for completeness' sake.

The second form of 'contemporaneity' is, however, more complicated since it involves the demand that the university help create for actual individuals a perfect present moment. In this position the demand is that the university be "relevant" to a very contemporary 'student' who, being without a past, is going to create *for himself* a perfect future – and right now! Since this present is strictly imaginary it becomes not contemporary but futurist. The advocates of individual relevance succeed then in showing what happens to the university when it becomes the servant of a utopian future. Three things are crucial in my criticism of this position. First, there is a displacement of a genuine anticipation of the future through the theoretical extrapolation of present knowledge. Second, the conception of individuality is unhistorical. Third, the desired present moment is only imaginary, involving a commitment to a sort of pseudo-eternity.

One of the very best definitions of this position is given by Harold Taylor who himself is only inconsistently sympathetic with it: "A radical in education is one who extends the limits of the curriculum beyond any set of ideas from anywhere and gives ultimate freedom to the individual psyche."[1] A more fulsome advocacy comes from Van Cleve Morris: "Whatever experiences in the school are most likely to arouse the individual's own private way of looking at life will be elevated to first position..."[2] Judson Jerome, another ambivalent advocate, puts it this way:

---

[1] Harold Taylor, *How to Change Colleges* (New York: Holt, Rhinehard and Winston, 1971), p. 28.
[2] Van Cleve Morris, *Existentialism in Education* (New York: Harper & Row, 1966) pp. 124–125.

Until Professors reorient themselves to the students they are hired to serve ... they [professors] will continue to be not only discontented, but burdened by a gnawing sense of irrelevance, insecurity and prostitution.[1]

Each of these statements is a strong expression of the important idea that universities are concerned with individuals. However, what results from the contemporary rediscovery of this concern is not merely a due regard for the student as a major focus of the encounter with the past and the present. Rather, the individual 'student' becomes the preoccupation of the university to the exclusion of even recognizing the *need* to make such encounters. The individual it seems is an individual *ab ovo* with neither a past nor a social present; he is somehow *only* a project, which is to say only his own future – his own enactment of *his* possibility.

It would be easy to substantiate that even though each of the last three authors I have mentioned tries to qualify his rediscovery of the student individual either in terms of the past or present, students who take that rediscovery to heart are interested in no such qualification. Surely almost every teacher has been encountered by a student who takes class time to demand that the course be relevant to *him* – him in the sense I have just mentioned. Indeed, this demand has been institutionalized at such *avante garde* colleges as Rochdale (Toronto) and Antioch-Columbia (Maryland), for example, in much the same way that Berkeley has institutionalized the research institute. On the other hand, St. John's College is a contemporary American version of an institution which adopts a monumental regard for the past as its primary concern. In any event, what I want to do is not substitute pre-occupation with the past for pre-occupation with the present and future. Instead, I am arguing that the university must care for all three of the moments in time in their integral unity.

[1] Judson Jerome, *Culture Out of Anarchy* (New York, Herder & Herder, 1971), p. 25.

V

Although other institutions in society may enact a concern for temporality, only the university is explicitly intended to do so. Thus it becomes crucial when that concern is attacked both from within and from without the university.

Given Heidegger's descriptions of temporality, it can be seen that Newman's monumental reverence for the tradition amounts to a dis-owning of temporality through instituting a care for the past in such a way that caring for the present and the future becomes impossible. In an analogous way Kerr's technological view of the university enshrines the present needs of society as the university's only legitimate moment of concern. Finally, the students' demand for individual relevance to their own future perfect moment is as disruptive of temporal continuity as the positions of Kerr and Newman.

Each of these forms of temporal blindness is of course manifest in the day to day activity of faculty and students. Monumental reverence for the past has always been with us. Kerr's technologism came upon us with the advent of World War II, and with the eager and active cooperation of faculty. In the view of Robert Nisbet, it is the complicity of faculty desiring to become the "new men of power" which is primarily responsible for the destruction of university community.[1] Discovered and admired by the society, academics decide that only the present moment is relevant. Thus given the establishment of the research institutes in the physical and social sciences wherein the power of the present is manifest, it was not long after that students, and then professors, in the humanities began to agitate for their own particular versions of disruption. Today it seems that one of the primary concerns of humanities faculties is the elaboration of techniques whereby their own social and economic presence may be recognized. Unionization thus becomes the temporal equivalent of the scientists' research institute in which only the present matters.

In my analysis, then, the university can be made whole

[1] Nisbet, esp. Chapter 6.

only if it rediscovers its temporal character. Yet I do not think this rediscovery will be an easy accomplishment. Faculty, students and society are aligned against it. Like Nisbet I am inclined to believe that the first move against the university's integrity was made by the faculty. Therefore, I think the first move of reconstruction must also come from faculty.

Several things can be done in this regard. In the first place, dialog on the nature of the university – rather than on its *uses* – must be reinstated. There is considerable evidence that this dialog has begun[1]; and although much of it takes the form of advocacy for one or the other of the temporally dis-ruptive positions I have described, still, when men continue to dialog, the possibility of clear sight remains. Secondly, given the analysis I have developed here it is possible to view the *apparently* separate activities of the academic disciplines as tied together by their specialized attention to one or the other moments of time. Given Heidegger's analysis, it then becomes subsequently possible to see those activities in their inherent interrelation. With such a view, it is further possible to see the complex activity of the modern university not as a disrupted multi-versity but as a temporal community in which classicist, engineer, and theorist exemplify care for time. After all, men do have a past, a present and a future; how fortunate it is then that there is a community in which care for each of these moments is institutionalized.

But caring for *each* of the moments of time may itself become a form of fragmentation if the unity of the concerns is not also emphasized. The principle guard against such fragmentation must lie in the hands of an administration which views these concerns with equal approbation. Such an administration must also insure that no single segment of the academic community succumbs to the belief that only its own work is the real purpose of the university. Now it seems to me that such administrative action is a necessary condition of the restoration of the university's temporal integrity. And such action is possible only for men who understand that

[1] See for example *Change*, a new journal devoted exclusively to discussions of higher education.

their acts are neither simply products of historical process nor simply independent of that process.

My paper, then, constitutes a recommendation to view the university in a specific way. With this view it is possible, I argue, to make the university whole again. In such a whole, tenure may be understood as *freedom from* that contemporaneity which demands that faculty ever be pre-occupied with the techniques of present survival or dependence. By the same token, academic freedom becomes the *freedom to* engage the temporality of man, either in its wholeness or in its various moments. Given the faculty acceptance of these responsible freedoms, it becomes clear that a society which endorses and supports the historical role of the university also endorses its own essential temporality – which is to say the possibility of its own free, responsible enactment. When the university serves its role of *being historical* it also serves the needs of students by continually reminding them of their own individual temporality. Thus, as with the medieval university, it is the task of university faculty not only to enact temporality but also through teaching to engage their students in that enactment. Only those who deprecate that enactment can exclaim 'the very idea of a university!'[1]

---

[1] The reflections in this article were first stirred by a question put to me in the Fall of 1967 by GEORGE BARTON when he asked me what the significance of HEIDEGGER's work was for educational theory. As with many good questions, often even the beginning of an answer is slow in coming.

THE ARGUMENT LAUGHS AT SOCRATES
AND PROTAGORAS

SHANNON DUBOSE

University of South Carolina

George Barton has been in the habit of teaching Plato by asking his students to find the place in a given dialogue where the philosophizing begins, and then showing them that nothing said in that dialogue is merely introductory. Rather, he makes them see that all of the conversation is germane to Plato's purpose in the dialogue.

The application of this method is particularly helpful in the study of the *Protagoras*, a dialogue which seems at first glance to be a comedy with philosophical interludes. There are no fewer than three layers of introductory conversation: Socrates talks to his unnamed friend (309); he recounts his early morning talk with Hippocrates (310–314); at length he introduces Hippocrates to Protagoras (316–318). At the end of the dialogue Socrates remarks that his sole object has been to investigate virtue (360e); the discussion of virtue, however, occupies only about eighteen Stephanus pages (329–334; 348–360), hardly more than one-third of the whole. If we add to that the examination of whether virtue can be taught (316b–328c, including Protagoras' long myth and the discussion of the merits of sophistry), we find that the clearly philosophical parts of the dialogue amount to somewhat more than half, that is, three-fifths of the entire *Protagoras*. No one could wish to dispense with the remainder of this sparkling conversation. One may wonder, though, whether Plato has for once been beguiled away from philosophy by the temptation to write comedy. Surely he parodies Prodicus (337a-c) and Hippias (337c–338a; 347b). Perhaps Plato parodies Socrates as well? Socrates' literary criticism (342–347) is rather preposterous than illuminating; he is caught by Protagoras in a false conversion (350); and he pouts when the argument does not go his way (334c–338).

This last point seems an especially clear sign that Socrates was not in serious pursuit of a philosophical inquiry, as an examination of the course of the dialogue will show. He threatened to cut short his conversation with Protagoras, on the plea that he had to keep an appointment (335c); at last he left with the same excuse (362). Plato makes a point of telling us, however, that no pressing business called Socrates away. In the exchange of pleasantries with which the *Protagoras* begins, Socrates has "just come" (310) from his set-to with the sophists. His friend begs him for an account of the proceedings, provided that Socrates has no other engagement. Making no reference now to his obligations, Socrates promptly settles down to talk.

Before dawn, says Socrates, he was roused by the young Hippocrates, come to beg an introduction to Protagoras. Socrates, well up on local news, adds that not only Protagoras, but also Hippias and Prodicus are visitors at Callias' house. He postpones calling until daylight, and occupies the interval by asking what Hippocrates expects to learn. Does he aim at professional or liberal education? Does Hippocrates really wish to become a sophist? Does he know whether what he is to learn will benefit or harm him? If one buys food from an itinerant trader, he can take it home in a separate vessel, so as to have its wholesomeness examined by a physician; but a doctrine learned is digested for good or ill (310–314).

At length day comes, and the two set out to see the sophists. With some difficulty they persuade a surly porter to admit them to the populous courtyard where Callias' visitors are already talking. Protagoras, Hippias, and Prodicus have each a coterie of admirers (314–315). Socrates recommends Hippocrates as a prosperous and intelligent pupil to Protagoras; Protagoras speaks to the antiquity of sophistry; the crowd gathers around Socrates and Protagoras; and the conversation with the sophists begins (316–318).

The ensuing discussion exhibits a number of arresting features. In the first place, the young Hippocrates, just introduced as a pupil and clearly an enthusiast, becomes a listener only, and says no more. There is, however, no dearth of speakers. Prodicus, Alcibiades, and Hippias, as well as Callias, Socrates, and Protagoras, all make contributions. The proceedings show remarkable variety. The contributors engage in speech-making as well as in question and answer. Protagoras and Socrates make long addresses; the oratory of Hippias and Prodicus in none the less pompous for being brief. Socrates cross-examines both Protagoras and Prodicus, and Protagoras cross-examines Socrates. Protagoras elaborates a myth; Socrates tries his hand at literary criticism and the history of philosophy. Socrates speaks for the many, while it is Protagoras who doubts their wisdom. Somehow, in the course of discussing the unity of virtue and whether virtue can be taught, Protagoras and Socrates exchange positions as well as opinions. Socrates says that if the argument had a human voice, it would laugh at them both (361a). Can all this have done Hippocrates any good?

Protagoras claimed that if Hippocrates came to him, he need endure no tiresome drudgery, but would still go home the first day a better man (318). Socrates undertook, he said, to speak for Hippocrates (318c), and expressed an earnest desire to learn from Protagoras (320b). Far from going home a better man, he seems to have become loquacious, captious, and even incoherent. To understand why, we must return to his cock-crow conversation with Hippocrates. There he urges Hippocrates to consume no untested food for the soul, and wishes for experts to examine the wholesomeness of doctrines before they are ingested (313–314). Socrates himself becomes the separate vessel (314a) into which the foreign matter is received; as he plays to the gallery, he lets Hippocrates observe the unwholesomeness of the product. If Protagoras' boast is justified, Socrates should present the picture of the successful pupil, made into a more virtuous citizen by the very first lesson. But Socrates is mischievous; by exaggeration he caricatures the position and method of Protagoras; Protagoras backs away from his early assertions and finally exchanges positions with Socrates (361ab). All this is done to show that sophistry does not improve the pupil, but rather corrupts him. It makes him long-winded, and he becomes a splitter of hairs, ready to ride rough-shod over his opponent.

Perhaps it will be well to show what Socrates finds worthy of parody in the sophists' talk.

Protagoras' first statement about sophistry (316c–317c) describes it as a practice which was ancient and widespread, but nonetheless concealed. Thus he claims Homer, Hesiod, Orpheus, Simonides, as well as assorted gymnasts and musicians, as members of his own profession who disguised their calling for fear of being known as sophists. Socrates' long speech (342–347) parodies these claims with his own analysis of Spartan and Cretan philosophy, representing their interest in philosophy as widespread, ancient, and concealed.

Among the Spartans, men and women, young and old enjoy philosophy. So as to give free expression to their philosophical zeal, at times they drive out foreigners and engage in a kind of philosophical orgy. The Spartans conceal their wisdom, preferring to give the impression that their preeminence is due to their fighting abilities.

They pretend to be ignorant, just because they do not wish to have it thought that they excel the other Hellenes by reason of their wisdom, like the Sophists of whom Protagoras was speaking... (342b).

At all times their philosophical excellence has made the Spartans politically supreme.

The antiquity of this brand of philosophy Socrates demonstrates by stylistic analysis: "Lacedaemonian brevity is the style of ancient philosophy" (343b). Among these laconic statements Socrates cites the Seven Sages' "Know Thyself" and "Nothing in Excess." He also quotes Pittacus' "Difficult it is to be good," the apophthegm which Simonides tackled in turn. Now Socrates moves on to parody Protagoras' statement that Simonides was a sophist. In order to do so, he first has a short exchange with Prodicus, whose disciple he claims to be (341a). The hair-splitting analysis of Simonides' ode which Socrates produces is worthy of Prodicus. It also constitutes Socrates' rejoinder to a view expressed by Protagoras in their first discussion of the unity of virtue: that to say two things are similar is not to say they are the same (331d). Socrates caricatures Protagoras' distinction by separating being from becoming in a way which follows the method of Prodicus and earns the congratulations of Hippias (who claims to be an expert on the ode in question: 347).

The central point of Protagoras' first recommendation of Sophistry seems to be that whoever teaches anything – music, gymnastics, poetry – teaches the same thing: sophistry. Socrates parodies this claim with his essay on Simonides and ancient philosophy. His effort is assisted by Prodicus and applauded by Hippias.

Protagoras' second claim is to his own preeminent ability to teach virtue: If Hippocrates comes to him, then he will go home the first day a better man, better able to handle affairs both private and public, in fact improved in political virtue. He promises to make good citizens (319a) and to do so without drudgery but with immediate results. Socrates objects that while the Athenians recognize experts in certain professions, and take advice from them, they allow all men to speak on matters of public policy; and, furthermore, that there are no recognized teachers of virtue. Protagoras does not reply by reverting to his earlier claim that all sorts of teachers are sophists who inculcate virtue. Rather, both his myth and his argument seem designed to show that all civilized men have a share of virtue, and that all teach virtue to one another. As he ends his long speech, Protagoras moderates his boast, saying that he believes himself one who is able to "promote virtue ever so little" more than others. In witness thereof he accepts his students' evaluation of his services (328bc).

If Socrates put himself in place of a pupil, he put no high value on Protagoras' tuition, since he found it less attractive than an apparently non-existent appointment, as we have seen. If Socrates was the 'separate vessel' in which food for Hippocrates' soul was tested, then the test is designed to show Hippocrates that Protagoras' claim is false. The fluency of the man who speaks at length does not guarantee that his matter is well thought out.

The fundamental principle upon which Protagoras' claim rests is the principle of the unity of virtue. Musicians, poets, gymnasts, all are sophists: they all teach the same thing. Not only that, all men teach virtue to one another. Protagoras does so more successfully than others, or so he says. He does so painlessly, not requiring drudgery of his pupils, not sending them back to disciplines such as mathematics, but teaching them political virtue directly and at once. In these assertions the unity of virtue is implicit. Protagoras' estimate of virtue is that to one who, like himself, has the knack, political virtue is simple in every sense of "simplicity": it is one thing, quickly and easily taught and learned. Moreover, in this great speech, Protagoras makes one clear assertion of the unity of virtue. Such evil qualities as injustice and impiety, he says "may be described generally as the very opposite of political virtue" (323e–324a). It is this assertion which Socrates takes up first in his cross-examination of Protagoras (328e–334c). The discussion of the unity of virtue begins with injustice and impiety. In the cross-examination, of course, Protagoras is unwilling to give his assent to the proposition that the several virtues are identical. As Socrates takes over and exaggerates the ground of Protagoras' claims, Protagoras himself shows a tendency to wish to draw distinctions. He hedges, and argues that it cannot all be quite as simple as Socrates wants to pretend. Despite his previous statements that everyone teaches virtue to everyone else (323c), he twice expresses doubts of the opinions of the many (333c, 351–353).

The second of the passages in which Protagoras doubts the wisdom of the many is the more interesting of the two because in it Socrates compels Protagoras to take popular opinion to be correct (358a) without considering whether the good might be defined in some other way. If identification of pleasure as the good seems an extraordinary doctrine for Socrates to put forward, it seems so because we fail to recognize that Socrates is playing mischievously with Protagoras' own notions. Socrates' examination of the belief that pleasure is the good results in advice to take up the study of reckoning in order to maximize pleasure (356). Learning virtue from Protagoras was to be a pleasant exercise, entailing no drudgery; most particularly it was not to require that the student return to the discipline of mathematics (318e). Socrates' humor is to require that Protagoras' pupil must calculate pleasure, and so to drive Protagoras and the company to see the unsteadiness of Protagoras' own ground.

Throughout the discussion with the sophists, Socrates caricatures his instructors. He tries to show Hippocrates – and whomever else it may concern – the sad effects of sophistry. Socrates the apt pupil pleases the sophists (340; 347; 361) even though he produces results which Protagoras the teacher finds indigestible in their exaggerated form. That virtue is one thing, that the many know it and teach it correctly are notions which in their full-blown form Protagoras comes to doubt. If Protagoras claims antiquity for sophistry, and discovers crypto-sophists among poets and prophets, Socrates can outdo him by discovering crypto-philosophers among the Spartans, and by producing an essay on Presocratic thought. If Protagoras protests that to say two things are similar is not to say they are the same, Socrates can outdo him in drawing distinctions to the satisfaction of Prodicus. Most important, if Protagoras claims to make men better at once, Socrates shows himself at his most mischievous. His long- windedness shows best in the disquisition on Simonides. His captiousness is also evident there. Having demanded that Protagoras keep his answers short (334–335), and threatened to leave unless his conditions were agreed to (335), Socrates soon begins to speak at length himself (342–347). For misinterpreting Protagoras' assertion about courage and confidence, Socrates shows no evidence of contrition (351), but simply changes the topic to pleasure and pain, developing a kind of utilitarianism. Having adopted this utilitarianism merely hypothetically (353b), he then rather rapidly decides to "substitute the names of pleasure and pain for good and evil" (355e), and goes on to conclude that "the pleasant is the good" without examining any other possibilities (358). This argument then becomes the basis for the identification of wisdom and courage (358d–360). By now Protagoras seems to have become too exhausted to protest further, and rather grudgingly agrees.

In his final speech Socrates admits that he has taken over Protagoras' ground, that Protagoras has moved to a Socratic position, and that the situation is laughable (361ab). Socrates does not confess that he has taken Protagoras' position mischievously. To do so would be to prevent the comic climax of the dialogue, in which Protagoras, echoing the approbation expressed earlier by Prodicus (340–341) and Hippias (347), offers his own earnest congratulations to an especially promising pupil (361e).

What Plato does in the *Protagoras* is to make an important point for the philosophy of education. He shows by caricature that sophistry lacks the merits that its proponents assert. The sophists cannot recognize excellence in discourse, and certainly they cannot teach it. Instead, they distort what was good in their pupils, and so endanger their pupils' integrity. Socrates aping his teachers provides both Hippocrates and the rest of us with an object lesson in the shortcomings of sophistry. When he says that his sole aim has been to investigate virtue, we should not understand Socrates to mean that he was pursuing the nature of virtue in a straight-forwardly serious way. He tells us that when he says that if the argument had a human voice it would laugh. The *aim* may be serious, but the investigation proceeds by an indirect route to reduce Protagoras' claim to an absurdity. Socrates' frivolous conduct is the example which shows that Protagoras taught folly. Thus the *Protagoras* is a comedy with a philosophical point.[1]

---

[1] Quotations are from the Martin Ostwald revision of the Jowett translation of the *Protagoras* in the Library of Liberal Arts (Indianapolis: Bobbs-Merrill, 1956). I have been strongly influenced by H. D. F. Kitto's able discussion of the *Protagoras* as drama in *Poiesis*, the Sather Classical Lectures, vol. 36 (Berkeley: University of California Press, 1966), although I do not always agree with his interpretation. I am grateful to Professor Rosamond Sprague for making several useful suggestions, which have enabled me to improve the exposition.

DEWEY AND DIALECTIC

FRANCIS E. GEORGE
Creighton University

This essay asks three questions concerning Dewey's philosophy and dialectical procedures: 1. How does Dewey ordinarily use the term dialectic? 2. Is there any sense in which Dewey's own philosophical method can be said to be dialectical? 3. Can some dialectical procedures effectively either criticize or contribute to the enterprise of philosophy as Dewey conceived it?

I

In a short article published in 1911, Dewey noted the uses of dialectic by Socrates, Kant and Hegel.[1] He also gave some indication that he thought dialectic, understood functionally, might be mildly useful in the construction of educational theory, at least in developing a theory of psychological alienation among adolescent students. As Dewey left his early Hegelian position and moved through the study of functionalist psychology into his major period of empirical naturalism, he became ever more severe in his judgment of dialectical methods. *Experience and Nature*, philosophically the most fundamental of Dewey's books, cites many philosophical errors which can be traced to the use of dialectical methods. The denotative method of Dewey's immediate empiricism operates entirely within experience, moving from primary non-reflective experience to secondary reflective experience and finally to reflectively enriched consummatory experience. Dewey's basic objection to dialectical method in philosophy, therefore, lies in its appeal beyond experience to

[1] "Dialectic," in *The Cyclopedia of Education*, Paul Monroe, ed. (Macmillan, 1911), Ib, Vol. II, 321–322.

an unexperienced condition of the possibility of experience or to an eventual outcome of experience which is non-continuous with present experience and therefore abstract. Dialectic thus produces transcendental theories incapable of verification. This methodological objection to dialectical procedures is the counterpart of Dewey's general rejection of metaphysical dualism. Nature and experience, matter and spirit, body and mind, man and God, object and subject, substance and process, person and community, fact and value – these traditional dualisms are so functionally interrelated that each is not just in the other but is genuinely of the other. Any philosophical method is tested by asking: "Does it end in conclusions which, when they are referred back to ordinary life-experience and their predicaments, render them more significant, more luminous to us, and make our dealings with them more fruitful?"[1] Since transcendental theories of reality help us only to escape from experience rather than to regulate the objects of experience in such a way as to further ideal goals within experience, the dialectical procedures which establish dualisms are philosophically pernicious.

Although he nowhere explicitly formulates a theory of dialectic, this general objection to the use of dialectical procedures in philosophizing enables us to distinguish several distinct ways in which Dewey uses the term. Dialectic can be considered (1) as a theory of meaning, (2) as an exercise in mental artistry, or (3) as a method of philosophical exposition and refutation.

1) Any theory of meaning is a theory of signs and signification. Charles Morris, who used Peirce's term "semiotic" to describe his general theory of signs in 1938, has recently described pragmatic semiotic as "the view that there is an intrinsic connection between meaning and action, such that the nature of meaning can be clarified only by reference to action."[2] Action is a term as ambiguous as meaning, and it

1 John Dewey, *Experience and Nature* (Chicago: Open Court Publishing Co., 1929, second edition), 7.
2 Charles Morris, *The Pragmatic Movement in American Philosophy* (New York: George Braziller, 1970), 16.

is only in the detailed application of the general pragmatic principle that Dewey's pragmatism takes shape and distinguishes itself from that of Peirce and James. But in every case, a behavioral or pragmatic semiotic finds cognitively valuable only those concepts which clearly signify a particular action. An inverse ratio obtains between a concept's cognitive usefulness and the scope of divergent experiential results it is supposed to signify.

Dialectic, according to Dewey, presents us with a theory of meaning in which, ideally at least, concepts and terms signify in a purely mental world with no possible reference to behavior or activities in the experiential manifold which Dewey calls nature. A mind operating entirely dialectically would be an entirely separate mind. Dewey, while rejecting the possibility of such a mind, imagines it as using a purely formal theory of meaning. Because a dialectical theory of meaning would have no existential referents, it could not function as a theory of inquiry. There would be no possibility of its concepts or terms being judged true or false. As Dewey states: "The principle of dialectic is identity; its opposite is not inconsistency to say nothing of falsity; it is nonsense."[1]

Dewey's rejection of a purely formal theory of meaning because a non-existential system cannot function as a theory of inquiry leads him to find all sorts of hidden physiological causes and social and moral purposes behind each use of dialectic by philosophers. Mistakes arise because of fatigue, because of a failure to see or hear correctly, or of a desire to get to the end of one's work or irrevocably defeat an opponent's argument. Thus, in practice, dialectic becomes an intellectual method which has an existential reference, but only to the psychological state of the philosopher. We deceive ourselves in imagining purely formal intellectual acts, when, as a matter of fact, there is no non-existential semiotic, no absolute distinction between psychology and logic. Dewey, of course, finds place for the distinction common in semiotic theories between denotation and meaning, between the extension and intension of a concept or term. But this dis-

---

[1] Dewy, *Experience and Nature*, 287.

tinction should not establish a separate mental world of meanings unrelated functionally to single natural events.

2) Because dialectic, as a theory of meaning, fosters inquiry independent of any possible verification procedures, it also engages the mind in constructing intellectual works of art. Rational meanings or essences produced dialectically by negating the transitory character of events can be easily contemplated by the philosopher. Certainly they are ideal objects of esthetic pleasure. Yet, for Dewey, even as they are appropriated and enjoyed as ends, such meanings cannot remain purely non-existential. They are had and used "in order to control better an eventual existential reference."[1] The uses of poetry, of religious ideals, of philosophical systems, are indirect and sophisticated, but such achievements enrich experience, always provided they are not taken to refer to transcendent objects antecedent to experience.

In pressing this point, Dewey turns dialectic against itself, making a dialectical argument against dialectic. He states that every use of dialectic ultimately appeals to some type of separated absolute which can be described only by analogy to events of ordinary experience. These events are then disparaged as mere appearance, in some sense unreal in relation to their absolute foundation – a foundation, which, to be itself, must appear "in a queer combination of rags and glittering gew-gaws, in the garb of the temporal, partial and conflicting things, mental as well as physical, of ordinary experience."[2] This existential contradiction, as Dewey calls it, is cited by him as evidence that any dialectical doctrine merely sorts out qualities and characters of things which naturally interpenetrate. Again, the fault lies not in the distinguishing, for mental art forms are as legitimate as any other and analysis is propaedeutic to inquiry and scientific discovery. The philosophical error arises in the argument to entities separate from nature merely because they are beautiful and we can enjoy them so.

---

[1] *Ibid.*, 289.
[2] *Ibid.*, 61. Cf. also, "The Intellectualist Criterion for Truth," in John Dewey, *The Influence of Darwin on Philosophy* (New York: Henry Holt and Company, 1910), 112–153.

3) In examining the dialectician's logical presuppositions and the consequences of his argument to see if they remain consistent with his stated position, Dewey shows himself a master of dialectic as a method of philosophical exposition and refutation. While careful never to rely upon dialectical argument to establish his own philosophical positions, Dewey is not slow to use it therapeutically, as did Socrates, to refute another position. The most cursory examination of his writings shows them filled with opinions he refutes by turning the arguments back upon themselves. This traditional use of dialectic is so obviously a standard tool of philosophers that Dewey once expressed surprise that it should be necessary to question his use of it.

In an exchange with Frederick J. E. Woodbridge, Dewey was accused by his Columbia University colleague of defending his theory of inquiry not on its own substantial merits but "by using it dialectically to confound every analysis of knowledge which implies an antecedent reality to which intelligence must conform in its operation if it is to be successful."[1] In effect, Woodbridge accuses Dewey of dialectical argument to a metaphysical position when Dewey states that knowledge must have practical consequences and then concludes from this premise that any object of knowledge must differ from the something experienced antecedent to the act of knowing. Woodbridge goes on to ask if Dewey's theory of inquiry, which is central to his philosophical views and to pragmatic philosophy in general, would be at all affected by the existence of antecedent objects of knowledge properly so called. Woodbridge thinks it would not; and, if not, why the endless pages of history and refutation of previous philosophical theses in Dewey's writings? Why does Dewey insist that only the *conclusion* of reflective inquiry can be said to be known, if his central thesis that knowing is an activity whose business it is to substitute controlled objects for perilous objects remains unchallenged whether or not objects are changed in their being known. Woodbridge finds the answer to his

[1] Frederick J. E. Woodbridge, "Experience and Dialectic," *Journal of Philosophy*, XXVII (May 8, 1930), 266.

question in an unexpressed but pre-supposed metaphysical position which consistently prefers the precarious to the stable. The thesis that only the consequents of scientific inquiry can be said to be known follows not from Dewey's theory of inquiry but from Dewey's process metaphysics. The defence of the thesis is dialectical, as are most metaphysical arguments, because the ground of the argument is conviction, not evidence.

In his response, Dewey first distinguishes subject matter to be known from objects of knowledge. He thereby again clarifies the mutual relation between experience and knowledge. He readily admits antecedent existences but denies identity between objects of direct experience and objects of knowledge as such. This position merely restates the distinction made in *Experience and Nature* between primary and secondary experience, a distinction most clearly worked out in terms of the theory of inquiry in the 1938 volume, *Logic, the Theory of Inquiry*. Having restated his position, Dewey answers the accusation that his method is dialectical rather than empirical: "Now, of course, I employ dialectic. I do not suppose that any one could write on philosophy without using it. If I could take the reader by the hand and lead him to see the same things I think I see and have the same experience I have, I would do it. Short of that possibility, I use dialectic. But this is ... obvious..."[1] Dialectic is employed only to bring others to see, not to demonstrate. The demonstration lies in the appeal to the procedures of the physical sciences. These change their objects in experimentation, and these operations and changes are empirical facts, not dialectical conclusions.

Beyond this purely expository use of dialectic, Dewey admits to the use of dialectic to refute a position itself frankly dialectical. Thus, in referring to Woodbridge's belief in stable substances, Dewey responds: "The history of thought seems to me to disclose that the belief in immutable existence is an emotional preference dialectically supported. Dialectic is obviously in place in dealing with a position as far as that

[1] John Dewey, "In Reply to Some Criticisms," *Journal of Philosophy*, XXVII (May 8, 1930), 273.

is itself dialectical. In any case, I have not meant to deny the theory of immutable substances because it is 'bad,' although it is pertinent to the dialectic to point out that bad consequences have resulted in morals and natural science from its assumption."[1]

To sum up, Dewey uses the term dialectic to denote (1) an inadequate theory of meaning, (2) a method of mental artistry which is enjoyable but non-cognitive, and (3), in the traditional sense, a method of philosophical exposition and refutation. Proof, as opposed to refutation, rests on empirical procedures. Since empirical method does not consist simply in observing states of affairs and reporting them, but moves beyond actual states of affairs in order to reconstruct them and control them, the procedure of reconstruction or hypothesis construction should be examined if Dewey's objections to dialectic are to be fully understood.

II

Reconstruction as a moment in the pattern of inquiry occurs in the determination of a problem-solution.[2] No situation is completely indeterminate for Dewey, and a careful observation and searching out of the constituent factors in a given situation will always suggest possible solutions. These solutions are imaginative extrapolations from a given state of affairs which is hypothetically reconstructed in such a way that the future event is satisfactorily controlled. Dewey calls this hypothetical reconstruction an idea. Its meaning lies in the anticipated consequences which are the future event. Ideas differ in intellectual value according to their clarity and their necessary relation to the event giving them meaning. A vague notion with no clear existential status is called a suggestion. Dewey explains: "The suggestion becomes an idea when it is examined with reference to its functional fitness, its capacity as a means of resolving

---

[1] *Journal of Philosophy*, XXVII (May 8, 1930), 274.
[2] Cf., John Dewey, *Logic: The Theory of Inquiry* (New York: Henry Holt and Company, 1938), 105–112.

the given situation."[1] A true idea functions so well that it contributes both theoretically and existentially to the reconstruction of a state of affairs. It is fully true as a constitutive factor in the future event.

This analysis of the relation between suggestion and idea does away with both the copy theory of ideas associated with classical empiricism and the Kantian synthesizing *a priori* structures, in particular the schemata of the imagination in which percepts and concepts are joined. For Dewey, the origin of concepts in percepts gives both an original functional correlativity with each other. Percepts locate and describe the problem while concepts describe a possible method of solution. Imagination plays a synthesizing role in reconstruction of a present state of affairs inasmuch as it provides experience vicariously and vicarious experience provides a base for an idea of a possible future event. An active imagination, according to Dewey, "is a sign that impulse is impeded and is grasping for utterance."[2] Imagination, while necessary for reconstruction, can also complicate the relation of future event to present idea. It can lead to a world of pure fantasy unrelated to present experience – the imaginative counterpart of a purely dialectical intellectual realm.

Rather than rely on subjective imagination as the connecting link between mere existence and fully meaningful reality, Dewey speaks of "the reflective relationship, the relation which an appearing object in its intrinsic qualities bears to the properties that capacitate it to be a sign of something else."[3] In every inquiry we take objects to be signs even when we are still uncertain as to what they are signs of. Inference is possible only if the object presented as evidence both retains its own primary qualities and also has an intrinsic relationship to something else still unknown. Inquiry is successful when the unknown object need no longer be symbolized by the evidence but can itself be enjoyed

---

[1] *Ibid.*, 110.

[2] John Dewey, *Human Nature and Conduct* (New York: Random House Modern Library, 1930), 153.

[3] John Dewey, "Appearing and Appearance," *Philosophy and Civilization* (New York: Minton, Balch and Co., 1931), 65.

rather than sought for. The reflexive relation between the sign and the signified remains, but their convertibility is now directly experienced.

Is this procedure dialectical? Despite Dewey's many writings on philosophical method, the question is complex and the answer not immediately clear. Dewey's theory of inquiry is explicit, but we have no clear model of dialectical procedures which can serve as a foil. When Dewey wrote of dialectic as a philosophical method, he seemed to have Hegelian dialectic in mind. But the use of dialectic by Hegel and by Bradley and other late nineteenth century Hegelians displays no single logical structure. As a method of explicating experience, its structure is as protean as experience itself.[1] As much as its origin in rationalism, this diversity of dialectic procedures is a forceful argument against the use of dialectic by those who demand a clear, consistent, and public methodology in philosophy. Nevertheless, despite the elusive character of dialectical procedures, three characteristics seem to be realized in any use of dialectic. As a philosophical method, dialectic is reflexive, teleological and inclusive.

As a method of refutation, dialectic looks for internal consistency in an argument. It analyzes unconscious assumptions and makes explicit all the consequences of assertions. The emphasis on internal consistency is carried further when dialectic is used as a method of discovery, for in this case an argument's lack of consistency with its own presuppositions or an existent object's failure to instantiate properly its own meaning or essence becomes the moving force of both inquiry and existence. In a word, dialectic is reflexive. But this characteristic alone would not serve to distinguish it completely from an empirical method such as Dewey's, which also moves from inadequate present fact to a possibility reflexively indicated in the present and finally to a

---

[1] Attention has been drawn to this difficulty in understanding Hegelian method by contemporary Hegel commentators. Cf., J. N. Findlay, *Hegel: A Re-examination* (New York: Collier Books, 1962), 68–79; Walter Kaufmann, *Hegel: A Reinterpretation* (New York: Doubleday Anchor Books, 1966), 153–162; and Jacob Loewenberg, *Hegel's Phenomenology: Dialogues on the Life of Mind* (La Salle, Ill.: Open Court Publishing Co., 1965), 15–22.

reconstructed future event continuous with present fact. Rather, what distinguishes dialectic is its insistence that the present existent fact is a negation of the possibility reflexively involved in it. Admittedly, what is actual is different both from what is merely possible and from a possibility which will be realized when what is now actual is so no longer; but the dialectician makes this negativity central to his method, so that negation is as real a characteristic of any state of affairs as is a quality positively denotable. This negation seems able to be more or less forceful; negation can take the logical form of simple otherness, of contrariety or of full contradiction, but the opposition thereby implied always involves, for the dialectician, some type of conflict.

The conflict-filled, initially negative situation is revealed as positive only when the resolution of the dialectic exposes conflict as a means to a more self-consistent end. Dialectic is teleological. Each logical and experiential difference is negated in turn, thereby exposing a larger, more inclusive continuous whole. This is done systematically and, according to classical readings of Hegel, necessarily. The movement from one stage of argument or development through its negation or destruction to a fuller system or greater synthesis is a process both logically necessary and existentially inexorable.

Negation, therefore, is a relation, uniting as well as separating its terms, and the goal toward which the dialectic moves is one of ever greater interrelatedness. The immanent rhythm of both thought and nature issues into a totality ever more integrated within itself. The Hegelian name for this totality is the Absolute. Teleology and inclusivity are seen finally as functions of the self-involving reflexivity which is the primary characteristic of dialectical method.

This abstract sketch of dialectical procedure brings to the fore not only salient differences but also some similarities with Dewey's theory of inquiry. First, there is a shared attitude. Dialectic is self-corrective, and Dewey's method of inquiry is designed to expose its own misuse. Secondly, dialectic is teleological; and Dewey explains that denotative method is purposive, since knowing is purposive and knowing participates in and is partially constitutive of nature. But because purpose remains known purpose and cosmic process is not telic, the development of a totally adequate and logically necessary system is not possible for Dewey. Thirdly, dialectic is inclusive; and Dewey's philosophical method seeks out continuity in natural events, without their ultimately culminating in an Absolute.[1] Lastly, both dialectic and reconstruction are reflexive processes. But while Dewey's reflexive relation supports organic interrelatedness, especially in his later transactional period,[2] it does not permit the philosopher to speak of negative facts. Thus, the incompleteness of any state of affairs (x), without its transactional correlatives (y and z), does not warrant our defining (x) as not-(y and z). Dialectical reflexivity, for its part, regards such definition as essential.

Despite some strong similarities, derivative mainly from Dewey's early Hegelian background, reconstruction is not a dialectical procedure. Should it be? Using dialectic in the only manner Dewey himself approved, we can ask if Dewey's philosophical methodology is adequate to his stated philosophical purposes. This question entails passing from formal structural comparisons to the pragmatic question of the usefulness of Dewey's method in constructing a philosophy of experience.

III

Are there experiences which a philosopher of experience should consider and which Dewey's method is not able to explicate? The most evident disagreement between dialectic and Dewey's method of inquiry lies in the interpretation of reflexivity. For Dewey, reflexivity involves interrelatedness but not negation, because there is no existential correlate of logical negation. The experiential status of negation thus becomes the issue on which the question turns.

---

[1] Cf., H. S. Thayer, *Meaning and Action: A Critical History of Pragmatism* (Bobbs-Merrill Company, Inc., 1968), 461 ff.

[2] John Dewey and Arthur F. Bentley, *Knowing and the Known* (Boston: Beacon Press, 1949), 121–123.

Dewey addresses himself to the relation between experience and negative propositions in the tenth chapter of *Logic: The Theory of Inquiry.* He makes two basic statements about affirmative and negative propositions: "(1) such propositions are functional in resolution of a problematic situation, and are (2) conjugate or functionally correspondent in relation to each other."[1] The function of negative judgment is not to report non-being, an utterly empty notion according to Dewey,[2] but to exclude certain facts or ideas from consideration in the attempt to transform an indeterminate situation into a determinate state of affairs. Negative propositions report the "existential experimental operative elimination"[3] of certain positive qualities which might possibly have aided the resolution of a problematic situation because it was hypothesized that they were reflexively involved in the situation. Comparison helps us to sort out the inconsequential from the telling in establishing evidence, and comparison is defined operationally. It involves turning to situations supposed to be logically similar but existentially different, and finding there clues for the successful resolution of the problematic case under study. For Dewey, change is the constant characteristic of experience, and negation is a logical function in a process of natural change. In a sentence which sums up the relation between negation and experience, Dewey explains: "'. . . the negative proposition as such formulates a change *to be* effected in existing conditions by operations which the negative proposition sets forth. It is an indication of experimental operation to be performed such that conditions will be so varied that the consequences of the operation will have an evidential significance lacking in the conditions as they existed at first."[4]

Dewey contrasts his functional position with both the Greek view that negative propositions indicate objective ontological

[1] Dewey, *Logic*, 181.

[2] Cf., Dewey's argument against Bradley in *Reconstruction in Philosophy*, enlarged edition (Boston: Beacon Press, 1948), 107 ff; and again in "Appearing and Appearance," *Philosophy and Civilization* (New York: Minton, Balch and Co., 1931), 56–76.

[3] Dewey, *Logic*, 183.

[4] *Ibid.*, 188.

deficiency in the subject of the proposition and with the modern view that negative propositions are purely formal. Non-being has been a theme of philosophical speculation since Parmenides stated that Being is, and Gorgias inferred that non-being is not. This early dialectic was expanded by Plato in the *Parmenides* and the *Sophist*. Plato suggests a reality of nothing as a ground of becoming and multiplicity. Dewey agrees that negation is connected with becoming but denies that nothing has an ontological status. Among modern philosophers of experience, Bergson explains away "the Nought" as a pseudo-idea, grounded in the displacement of one being by another. The lazy thinker generalizes from this experience and then supposes that negation has equal status with affirmation because they are verbally similar. Bergson writes: "... for a mind which should follow purely and simply the thread of experience, there should be no void, no nought, even relative or partial, no possible negation."[1] Of course, a mind endowed with memory passes beyond this crude positivism to noting the disappearance of things and to the construction of the notion of possibility. Since the disappearance of everything including the nought is impossible, the nought is exposed as a self-destructive notion, a pseudo-idea. For Heidegger and Sartre, on the other hand, negation has experiential status in itself rather than as a moment in a process of change. Particularly in the analysis of self-transcendence and self-creation through the experience of nothingness, dialectical procedure becomes again a critical issue in contemporary philosophy.

If the experience of one's subjectivity is unique, the continuity needed both for comparison with other selves and for reflexivity between self and environment would be lacking. Ordinary or typical experience is repeatable and continuous, but in limit situations the self has nothing with which to compare its experience and it comes to terms with itself alone. The limit experience is unique. It is neither problematic, because no satisfactory resolution is possible; nor is it esthetic or consummatory, since it is unenjoyable. Traditionally, the

[3] Henri Bergson, *Creative Evolution* (New York: Random House Modern Library, 1944), 319.

anticipation of death has forced the self back upon its own subjectively unique individuality. But other limit situations can perhaps serve as well to illustrate negation within experience. Thus, historical events, each unique and each having ceased to be, present a challenge to Dewey's method of inquiry. Dewey, Mead and Randall treat the past as functionally related to present experience, but in so doing they attenuate the distinction between the remembered past which is autobiographical and the historical past which is the subject of study by historians.

Again, reflection on the self in the experience of knowing exposes an area of self-consciousness which is paradoxically both private and yet self-transcendent. In knowing, the knower can reflexively experience himself as the limit of the object, as what the object known is not. This awareness of negation establishes the distinction between the knower and the known in the act of knowing. While this experience, as Dewey insists, is not of great importance for scientific knowledge as such, it nevertheless opens to discourse the entire realm of subjectivity. The world-constituting and world-alienating self in isolation from cultural and social contexts is rightly the object of Dewey's scorn,[1] but the distinction between activity and object in any situation remains important even in Dewey's functional analysis. Since Dewey admits that reality cannot be reduced to what is object for a subject, a total transactional analysis would seem to demand an investigation of that component of a situation which cannot adequately be an object for itself and which yet retains a sense of itself in the experienced situation.

Once the experience of negation in limit situations is located and defined dialectically, how can it be responded to? One form of speaking about both history and subjectivity is the myth. In Plato's dialogues, for example, myth and dialectic are inextricably intertwined, because nothing in the dialogue can be taken literally. In non-literal discourse the subject speaking myth (mythologizing) transcends his own limits without separating himself from his experience. Using non-literal or symbolic language, the myth allows the empiri-

[1] Dewey and Bentley, *Knowing and the Known*, 142, footnote 20.

cally unique to happen many times. It establishes a relation
between language and events which enables the speaker to
attribute significance to an experience not comparable to other
events and therefore not totally explicable by reference to
them.

Besides the historical past and the subjective self, both
of which have been the subject of much philosophical speculation, a contemporary example of mythologization, of generalization from a limit situation without empirical comparison,
can be had in eco-consciousness. The image of the earth as
seen from the moon, an image which itself participates in the
reality it represents, can evoke an experience of both parti-
cipation and transcendence. Nature as a whole becomes an
object of experience. Inquiry into nature as a whole leads to
the scientific conclusion that the finite global system cannot
endure continued exponential growth. This conclusion brings
into focus a limit situation. The possibility of the collapse of
nature as a system would entail the end of experience, since
for Dewey nature and experience are convertible. On one level,
this threatening situation is a problem and can be handled by
scientifically anticipating the consequences of our present way
of life. But on another level the criticism of all the conditions
of experience, of the entire eco-system, transforms experience
and moves us to a more inclusive order in which nature as a
whole, since it can be negated, can also become an object of
philosophical wonder.

The use of negation to lead the philosopher beyond the
context of Dewey's naturalism does not establish dialectic
as a method of proof; but it does suggest that the philosopher of experience should be prepared to use as many methods
as experience itself demands and that dialectic can be useful
in locating and clarifying experiences of negation. The logical
looseness of dialectic, its seeming ability to serve any purpose
and prove any point, demands great caution in its use, even
as a means of evoking and then defining negative dimensions
of experience in limit situations. Nevertheless, Dewey himself
used dialectic to force others to see the consequences of their
philosophical arguments; and the further use of dialectic to
force others to see areas of experience which present peculiar

problems for philosophers would seem to be legitimate. Dewey's objection to Hegelian dialectic, as he seemed to understand it, exposes it as an attempt to deal with change and process in a non-empirical fashion. For Dewey, Hegelian dialectic concentrated on the negation logically connected with any report of change, because negation can be treated using non-empirical or purely logical methods. But the dialectical procedure discussed in the third part of this essay does not attempt to deal with change. It attempts to come to terms with limit situations, with a type of experience which is negative but without development. In such situations we can neither adequately systematize our experience nor completely resolve our conundrums. As a method of inference, dialectic is inadequate; but dialectic is also a form of discourse which attempts to deal with paradoxical modes of consciousness. To the extent our experience is not just problematic but paradoxical, dialectic can serve philosophy without forcing it into transcendental metaphysics.

EXPERIENCE AS REVELATORY OF NATURE
IN DEWEY'S METAPHYSICAL METHODOLOGY

JOHN G. JARDINE
Wilkes College

Dewey's approach to philosophical methodology was, it scarcely needs saying, empiricist. In common with all empiricists (in so far as they were empiricists), he rejected as meaningless any upper-case Reality which transcends the conditions of spatio-temporal experience and any "faculty," like upper-case Reason, of attaining such a Reality. One of the characteristics of empiricism, however, is that it appears to rob man of so much that he considers valuable. In Hume's empiricism, especially, the world and man seem to disintegrate into a sand storm.

Once we free our minds from such distortions of Dewey's thought as, for example, that it is narrow scientism and American commercialism gone academic, he is seen to be less of the philosophic robber baron who steals the ground from beneath us than most other empiricists. Dewey was a highly critical philosopher, but he continually spoke of reconstruction rather than destruction. Dewey's metaphysical universe is packed and rich. Dewey was convinced that philosophies of experience which robbed the world of its colors, sounds, beauty, novelty, and value – of its dance of life – were inadequate *simply because* they robbed the world of what was genuinely experienced. A "first rate" test for the validity of any philosophy, according to Dewey, is this:

Does it end in conclusions which, when they are referred back to ordinary life-experiences and their predicaments, render them more significant, more luminous to us, and make our dealings with them more fruitful? Or does it terminate in rendering the things of ordinary experience more opaque than they were before, and in depriving them of having in "reality" even the significance they had previously seemed to have.[1]

---

[1] *Experience and Nature* (New York: Dover Publications, 1958; reprint of second, 1929, edition), p. 7.

Dewey's empiricism, meant to illumine the world of everyday life, is critical not only of rationalism but also of most empiricisms. For Dewey a philosophy of experience must state what the world is experienced *as*, not explain away what it is experienced as, and it is primarily experienced as a qualitative world. The restoration of the qualitative is, indeed, one of the most remarkable features of Dewey's philosophy. The significance of this will be drawn out later.

For Dewey philosophy begins and ends in experience. Metaphysics, too, if it is to be a meaningful enterprise, must begin and end in experience. Nevertheless it is not correct to interpret Dewey as a philosopher of experience if we think of a philosopher of experience as one who believes that what we confront in experience *is* experience, e.g., what we perceive is perceptions. Dewey insists that we do not experience experience but rather experience nature.[1] It is accordingly impossible to consider adequately Dewey's interpretation of experience apart from his interpretation of nature. For Dewey what is experienced is genuinely revelatory of nature.[2]

The experience of nature is not, however, identical with the knowledge of it; for this reason I have used the vague term "revelatory" to suggest the relationship between experience and nature. "Revelatory" suggests a certain immediacy of content, which is what Dewey was driving at. For Dewey, knowledge takes place *within* experience and represents a special way of handling experience. Knowledge is derivative rather than original, and, accordingly, the "objects" of knowledge are derivative rather than original.[3] Dewey considered the identification of the objects of knowledge with the "really real" to be a basic philosophic fallacy, indeed, *the* philosopher's fallacy. What is "really real" is what is experienced. Knowledge gives an account in terms of antecedents and consequences of what is experienced; it brings understanding to experience. The objects of knowledge are important in understanding what is experienced, but they do not do away with

---

[1] *Ibid.*, p. 4a.

[2] *Ibid.*, pp. 3a, 19–20.

[3] *Ibid.*, pp. 23ff. On the notion of object as derived, see *Logic: The Theory of Inquiry* (New York: Henry Holt and Company, 1938), p. 119.

what is experienced nor are they more ultimate or more real.[1] Experience is not subsumed in knowledge, but rather knowledge is subsumed in experience. We can "explain" water as H_2O, but water is, in primary experience, what we wash in, drink, sail on, and the like. To suppose that to interpret water as H^2O makes less real the features we experience is nonsense.[2] If anything, the knowledge of water as H_2O makes it possible to enlarge our experience with it (e.g., electrolyzing it to produce oxygen).

The drive behind Dewey's subordination of knowledge to experience is not a crude practicalism but rather a concern for the integrity and wholeness of experience. His empiricism is anti-reductionist. His stress on "continuity" arises out of the effort to return to the integrity and wholeness of experience. The continuity within experience is not only spatial but temporal, indeed, mainly temporal. An experience does not happen all at once but rather has temporality as an essential constituent of its happening. But an experience is revelatory of nature, not a self-enclosed state, and so nature, too, is essentially spatio-temporal. Nature is not given all at once but has temporality as an essential constituent. Nature is not a thing but a happening.[3]

Dewey attempted to integrate experience and nature intimately by interpreting experience behavioristically, as far as possible, and dropping out, as far as possible, the association of experience with conscious states, or, more exactly, with subjective states. He accordingly defined experience as "things interacting in certain ways."[4] In common idiomatic English usage this is somewhat unusual but not completely so. For example, we can say, "Wilkes-Barre experienced its worst flood in its history in the summer of 1972." We are not so

[1] *Experience and Nature*, p. 5.

[2] *Ibid.*, pp. 193–194.

[3] Dewey, *Logic*, p. 220; *Experience and Education* (New York: Macmillan, 1938), pp. 27, 42; *Intelligence in the Modern World: John Dewey's Philosophy* (ed. with an intro. by Joseph Ratner, New York: The Modern Library, 1939), p. 1050. "The Need for a Recovery of Philosophy," in Richard J. Bernstein, ed., *John Dewey on Experience, Nature, and Freedom: Representative Selections* (New York: The Library of Liberal Arts, 1960), pp. 23, 25, 27–30, 63; *Experience and Nature*, pp. x–xii, 4a–1 [sic].

[4] *Experience and Nature*, p. 44.

much focusing primarily on the conscious states of the Wilkes-Barrians as we are on the *event* of considerable water flooding Wilkes-Barre.

Immediately after saying that "things interacting in certain ways *are* experience" Dewey adds that such things "are what is experienced" – in other words, he shifts from an active tense to a passive tense, which seems to move the experience of things to another active center. "Linked in certain ways with another natural object – they are *how* things are experienced as well."[1] This other natural object is the human organism. Dewey's highly compressed formula seems to suggest that in the human organism, experience (which is primarily an inter-action among things) becomes *aware* of itself. The thrust of these remarks is to insist that experience is part of nature, that it is *in* nature, and that it is *of* nature. Experience is continuous with nature, reaching into its length, breadth, and depth. Experience is

an affair of the intercourse of a living being with its physical and social environment . . . . What experience suggests about itself is a genuinely objective world which enters into the actions and sufferings of men and undergoes modifications through their responses.[2]

Dewey's philosophy of experience is hence fundamentally realistic. And his emphasis on existence-as-interaction brings with it the assertion that experience is charged with con-tinuities, connections, and involvements. "An experience that is an undergoing of an environment and a striving for its control in new directions is pregnant with continuities and connections."[3] But since experience is of nature, nature is pregnant with continuities, connections, and interactions. The continuities, connections, and interactions of experience and nature are not only spatial but also temporal. Inference, therefore, is not an artificial constituent of experience; it is, indeed, the stretch of experience. But if experience contains inference as an essential constituent, nature too contains a kind of inference, a kind of temporal continuity not only

[1] *Ibid.*
[2] "The Need for a Recovery in Philosophy," in Bernstein, p. 23.
[3] *Ibid.*

binding past to present but present to future. Experience accordingly is not a veil or film over nature but seeps into it. To speak of the characteristics of experience, then, is to speak of the characteristics of nature (as it presents itself to experience). Experience, specifically human experience, which includes reflective consciousness, is, therefore, the "growing progressive self-disclosure of nature itself."[1] Hence it is that one must take the qualitative factors presented in experience seriously.

Dewey pressed hard in his insistence of the intimate interweaving of experience and nature. To give some examples which show how thoroughly he accepted this interweaving: Doubting is often considered a purely subjective state. The situation is supposed to be just what it is, *i.e.*, a definite structure. It is *we* who are confused. All we must do is, subjectively, to resolve doubt and see the situation for what it is. Dewey, on the other hand, stated that we "are doubtful because the situation is inherently doubtful."[2] Doubtfulness is a quality of certain of our experiences revelatory of a genuine existential condition. Certain features of the world *are* doubtful. Likewise certain features of the world are genuinely fearful. Fear is not a purely subjective feeling or quality. Fear is a "function of the environment. Man fears because he exists in a fearful, an awful world. The *world* is precarious and perilous."[3] And if

experience actually presents esthetic and moral traits, then these traits may also be supposed to reach down into nature, and to testify to something that belongs to nature as truly as does the mechanical structures attributed to it in physical science.[4]

The qualitative features of existence presented to us in experience, then, are real features of existence.

These texts may appear to suggest that Dewey advocated a naive and uncritical acceptance of experience at its face value. This would be to misinterpret what Dewey is driving

[1] *Experience and Nature*, p. x.
[2] *Logic*, pp. 105–106.
[3] *Experience and Nature*, p. 42.
[4] *Ibid.*, p. 2.

at. Indirectly he was criticizing any conception of method which starts off with a general doubt about the validity of experience. Specific doubts may, however, be valid, if their foundations and possibility of resolution occur within experience. Since experience is the only way by which nature is revealed to us, the presumption is in favor of what experience presents itself as immediately, unless there are specific ambiguities and conflicts within experience which suggest that things are not quite what they seem or that there is more than what immediately strikes the eye.

The acceptance of the validity of experience is consistent with the theory of evolution. The way man experiences arose out of responses to the environment; man's experience adapts him to his world, and it is difficult to see how man could have evolved means of adaptation which have no connection with the world in which he lives and to which they adapt him. Rather the presumption is in favor of the view that experience is connected to the world in which it arises and revelatory of the world. The real justification of experience lies not in the theory of evolution, however, but in its here-and-now capacity to fruitfully bring about adjustment of man to the world, which is primarily the world of man – the social, political, economic, ethical, and cultural world. The theory of evolution is itself derivative, an interpretation of experience, such that experience first justifies the theory of evolution, and the theory of evolution then turns back upon and helps illumine the nature of experience.

There is another significant "anti-Cartesian" trait that might be noted here. Descartes had insisted that thought should progress from the simple and work its way to the complex. Many philosophers, since and even before Descartes, attempted to seek out the ultimate "simples" out of which the complex world is supposedly constituted. Now, if experience is anything, it is complex, far from clear and distinct. Furthermore, the presumption in favor of simples tends to terminate in the assertion that the simples are the ultimately Real and that the complex is derivative. It is, therefore, no wonder Descartes was suspicious of the revelatory value of experience.

Dewey rejected the assertion that we should start with

simples and from them derive the complex. "Suppose that ...
we start with no presuppositions save that what is experienced,
since it is a manifestation of nature, may, and indeed must
be used as a testimony of the characteristics of natural
events."[1] Hence reveries, desires, "the possibilities present in
imagination that are not found in observations," the "features
of objects reached by scientific or reflective experience," "the
phenomena of magic, myth, politics, painting, and penitent-
iaries," the "experience of ignorance as well as of wisdom, of
error and even insanity" "are pertinent for a philosophic
theory of the nature of things ...." Social life, usually
ignored by metaphysicians, especially those in quest of
"simples" is highly relevant to the "problem of the relation
of the individual to the universal," at least as relevant as the
data of logic.

The existence in political organization of boundaries and barriers,
of centralization, of interaction across boundaries, of expansion and
absorption, is quite as important for metaphysical theories of the discrete and the continuous as is anything derived from chemical analysis.[2]

Dewey was not saying that all these phenomena are real *in
the same way* but that they are all relevant for an interpretation of reality. There are no *a priori* criteria for excluding
phenomena as irrelevant. In specific inquiry we eliminate
certain phenomena and concentrate on others, but this process
is valid for the *specific* inquiry at hand and is not necessarily
universalizable beyond its bounds. It is a fallacy to suppose
what is ignored in a specific inquiry does not exist or cannot
form the subject matter of another specific inquiry. The
integrity of experience has suffered, as has been noted, with
the identification of the objects of knowledge with the real.
A great deal of reality has thereby been ignored, at cost to
metaphysics.

... nature is construed in such a way that all these things [e.g.,
dreams, logic, social life, madness], since they are actual, are naturally
possible; they are not explained away into mere "appearance" in

[1] *Ibid.*, pp. 19–20.
[2] *Ibid.*

contrast with reality. Illusions are illusions, but the occurrence of illusions is ... a genuine reality. What is really "in" experience extends much further than that which at any time is known. ... Whenever the habit of identifying reality with the object of knowledge as such prevails, the obscure and vague are explained away. It is important for philosophic theory to be aware that the distinct and evident are prized and why they are. But it is equally important to note that the dark and twilight abound. ... Things are objects treated, used, acted upon and with, enjoyed even more than things to be known. They are things had before they are things cognized. ... Cognitive experience must originate within that of a non-cognitive sort.[1]

Experience is primarily "action-undergoing."[2] Action and undergoing are, however, serial things. When one acts or undergoes (actually both occur together in experience; each experience is both an action and an undergoing), time is required for their happening and execution. Time is crucial for the notion of experience. An organism is concerned with what it is doing and what is happening. Its preservation depends on its ability to organize its future in its favor, since its existence is temporal. "Organic functions deal with things as things in course, in operation, in a state of affairs not yet given or completed."[3] The adjustment of an organism to its environment

takes time ...; every step in the process is conditioned by reference to further changes. ... In so far as the issue of what is going on may be affected by intervention of the organism, the moving event is a challenge which stretches the agent-patient to meet what is coming.[4]

Organisms essentially move forward, and hence experience is a "future implicated in a present."[5] Hence it is that "experience ... is experimental, an effort to change the given; it is characterized by projection, by reaching forward into the unknown; connection with the future is its salient trait."[6]

---

[1] *Ibid.*, pp. 20–21, 23.
[2] *Ibid.*, p. 23; *cf.* "The Need for Recovery in Philosophy," in Bernstein, pp. 23–26, 45.
[3] "The Need for a Recovery in Philosophy," in Bernstein p., 33.
[4] *Ibid.*, p. 26.
[5] *Ibid.*
[6] *Ibid.*, p. 23.

But as experience is not isolated from nature, but interacts with it, nature too is characterized by a thrust into the future; it is experimental. Change and the emergence of new configurations are essential to nature.

The future thrust of experience and nature is not a subordination of the present (which includes the past) to the future. Rather it is to say that the character of existence *now*, for it to be what it is *now*, is to be future-implicating. To be *as* a serial being requires the ability to come to grips with the future. In Dewey's earlier mature writings he seemed to subordinate the present, and especially the past, to the future. This was, in part, because he was concerned with giving an instrumentalist reading of knowledge, which stressed future-referential consequences. He was also concerned with problem-solving actions, especially of an ethical and educational nature, which evidently entails a future reference. Any ethical theory, since it is concerned with choices necessary for the good life, must be concerned with the future, for that is "where" choices have their impact. Education, similarly, is concerned with the impact of present influences on future patterns of behavior.

However, in Dewey's most mature thought he attempted to correct the overly instrumentalist reading of experience by insisting that experience, in addition to its instrumental phases, also has certain consummatory phases, some of which are of utmost preciousness, to which other experiences are instrumental. Art, for example, possesses such consummatory qualities, and Dewey strenuously protested against its subordination, especially to commercialism. The highest consummatory experience for Dewey is that of face-to-face human association in a meaningful, enriching community. But if art and meaningful human association are consummatory, it does not mean that they are static. Duration with continual variation is of their essence. What is the experience of a poem, of a film, of a painting, of pleasant conversation, of a sexual encounter, without such duration? An experience disintegrates when it loses its thrust. A world without dynamic thrust hence is no world at all, and a world with thrust is one in which past, present, and future belong to its constitution.

Dewey, as we have seen, refused to consider experience and knowledge as coextensive. Knowledge, however, is not something other than experience but is a kind of experience. It is experience which has a certain kind of meaning. Knowledge is not coextensive with meaning, nor is meaning coextensive with experience, although no meaning is *a priori* exempt from being a subject of inquiry (esthetic experience, for example, can be dealt with "scientifically" although the experience is not science nor reducible to science) and no experience is *a priori* exempt from meaningfulness. The meaning of a thing is its *import*, either instrumental or consummatory or both. For Americans, the American flag may mean – have the import – that they are free, but it is quite another matter to say that it is *true* that they are free. Truth and falsity are those meanings which are associated with future consequences, with connections which are verifiable. Hence if Americans are free, then the consequences associated with freedom must be operative for the statement to be true; if they are not operative, then the statement is false. The statements of metaphysics cannot escape the demand of future operability. They are true if in each experience they are borne out inescapably. Hence the statement that change belongs to the structure of existence is true if in any experience which will or can take place change will be experienced as an irreducible feature.

Experience is, therefore, patterned and patternable, connected and connectable – so, likewise is nature. In the patternability and connectability of experience and nature, in the openness of experience and nature lies the possibility of creative intelligence.

Experience cannot be reduced to immediate, fleeting, self-contained sensation. When I look at a person, a chair, or a building, I do not simply "see" extended colors. I "see" – experience – a person, a chair, or a building. Experience is denser, richer, and more extensive than simple sense-data. Indeed, there are no simple sense data; or, rather, simple sense-data are an abstraction of features intimately involved with a more packed experience. Interpretation belongs to human experience as connection belongs to nature; indeed, the two are continuous with one another. There is no experience without interpretation, and interpretation is not a purely private affair, my interpretation. Just as experience is a public affair, not something which occurs exclusively in a subject, so "my" interpretation of experience and nature found in philosophy, religion, science, art, institutions, laws, culture and the like are public, at least in principle. These interpretations are not just "here" but have projections into the past out of which they arose. Hence any analysis of experience brings with it historical inquiry into its interpretation, as it includes imaginative projections of possibilities for the future. This, it seems to me, is central to Dewey's conception of philosophic method; why philosophic method, concerned with interpreting experience and clarifying its implications and possibilities, must have an historical dimension.

Dewey has often been criticized as being anti-historical. That Dewey was frequently unfair to the past, especially past thought, or sometimes misinterprets events, may well be true, but even if true, it does not follow that Dewey was anti-historical. Dewey had little patience with antiquarian history, the study of the past simply for its own sake, with no reference to the present and the future. A philosopher critical of an antiquarian approach to the past is not, however, thereby anti-historical. In fact, too great a concern with the past, too great an effort to bear the weight of the past, as Nietzsche has pointed out (in the *Use and Abuse of History*) stands in the way of life – and it might be added, of history.

Dewey located history here-and-now, in the present doings and sufferings of men. Few philosophers have concerned themselves with history in this sense as did Dewey. Dewey concerned himself with past doings and sufferings only in so far as he believed they were relevant for good or ill to the present and to the future. This concern was considerable, since he believed in the continuity between past and present. In Dewey's educational writings, for example, are several explicit discussions of the educational value of history (e.g., the little jewel entitled "The Aims of History in Elementary Education" in *The School and Society* or "The Significance of Geography and History" in *Democracy and Education*), which indicate that Dewey placed considerable value on history. And in nearly all of his writings are discussions of the past, so many indeed that if they were removed, his writings would shrivel considerably, perhaps by half, and their coherence would disintegrate. In a work like *Experience and Nature* we find a constant interweaving of philosophic and historical analysis.

What this blending of philosophy and historical analysis suggests is that Dewey did not separate the two, that the historical analysis belongs to Dewey's conception of philosophical analysis. Dewey's conception of philosophy commits it to an analysis of the concrete, which includes the present state of philosophical analysis, a state dependent, often deplorably so, on its past. An analysis of the concrete cannot be done with "eternal" and "necessary" dialectical categories, but must be done through an analysis of experience as it presents itself in experience, the present tense of which includes a past tense (and also a future tense); the concrete is tensional.

The history of philosophy represents an ongoing criticism and interpretation of experience. The interpretation given by past philosophies does illumine experience and nature, but these interpretations also distort and misunderstand it. Hence the effort to construct a more adequate interpretation of experience and nature entails a critical interpretation of the history of philosophy, even more, a critical analysis of the history of culture. Philosophy accordingly cannot escape he necessity of social inquiry if it is to be genuinely critical. Interpretation, like experience and nature, with which it is continuous, is historical.

If there is a continuity between experience and nature, if experience is genuinely revelatory of nature, if knowledge is essentially grounded on experiential, consequential verifiability, if metaphysics attempts to give knowledge of the generic, or irreducible, traits of existence (*i.e.*, experience and nature), it follows that only empirical method is valid and adequate for metaphysics; empirical method, however, is inseparable from historical method. The ground of this inseparability is finally that experience and nature are radically historical. Dewey's methodological commitments culminate in a metaphysics of process, of emergence. To be sure, this means loss of the Absolute and its assurance. "A free man," wrote Dewey in *Human Nature and Conduct*, "would rather take his chance in an open world than be guaranteed in a closed world."

DEWEY AND THE BEHAVIORAL THEORY OF MEANING

HAROLD N. LEE

Tulane University

I

A dominant theme of Dewey's book *The Quest For Certainty*[1] is his opposition to the "spectator theory of knowledge" which Western philosophy inherited from the Greeks. According to the spectator theory the "office of knowledge is to uncover the antecedently real" (QC 17). Dewey would substitute what he variously calls the experimental, the instrumental, or the operational view of the nature of knowledge. Dewey regards knowledge as a mode, albeit a very complex one, of action, behavior. "Knowing is itself a mode of practical action and is *the* way of interaction by which other natural interactions become subject to direction" (QC 107, italics Dewey's).

Dewey's opposition to the spectator theory was apparent long before he delivered the Gifford lectures which were published as *The Quest For Certainty*. It is the core of the argument in Chapter IV of *Experience And Nature*.[2] The fourth essay in *The Influence Of Darwin On Philosophy And Other Essays* entitled "The Experimental Theory of Knowledge" foreshadows the clear-out distinction between the two views of the nature of knowledge and it was originally published in 1906.[3] Dewey used the term "instrumental knowledge" and "instrumental character of thinking" as early as 1903,[4] and the de-

---

[1] John Dewey, *The Quest For Certainty* (New York: Minton, Balch & Company, 1929) p. 23. This title will be hereinafter cited QC with the page number.

[2] John Dewey, *Experience And Nature* (Chicago: The Open Court Publishing Company, 1926), Hereinafter cited EN with page number.

[3] John Dewey, *The Influence of Darwin On Philosophy And Other Essays* (Bloomington: Indiana University Press, 1965), pp. 100–101. First published in 1910. Hereinafter cited ID with page number.

[4] John Dewey, *Essays In Experimental Logic* (New York: Dover Publications,

velopment of the instrumental theory was a phase of the evolutionary naturalism that became dominant in Dewey's thought as he left his early Hegelianism. The spectator theory follows from the Greek view of a static, unchanging Reality of substance and essence. Hegel rejected the static Reality in favor of time, history, process, but his view remained rationalistic. After Darwin, however, history and development could be naturalized in an evolutionary world. Mind and knowledge could be looked at as factors in human adaptation and survival instead of being rationalistically regarded as psychical and extra-natural. In this growing naturalistic conviction Dewey was strongly influenced by William James' *Principles of Psychology*, published in 1890, even though James' views in the *Principles* were not unequivocally naturalistic.[1] Knowledge, for Dewey, became a tool for solving problems of adaptation and control of man's environment.

One of the most characteristic features of American pragmatism in general is its rejection of the assumption that knowledge is the assimilative grasp of what is antecedently real, and that the ideal of perfect knowledge and the goal of all knowledge is the contemplative vision of Being.[2] For any philosophy significantly called pragmatic, knowledge is a way of reacting – a way of meeting and coping with the environment. Each of the early pragmatists had his own version of this doctrine. Dewey usually called his variation "instrumentalism," though he also used the word "experimentalism." In *The Quest For Certainty* he often called it "operationalism."[3] No matter the name, the import is clear: the data of experience pose a problem. How are they to be responded to? How is the problem to be met? What reaction or series of reactions will set the data in order and alter them in such a manner as to solve or contribute to

Inc., 1953) pp., 174–175, First published in 1916. Hereinafter cited EEL with page number. The essay referred to was originally published in the 1903 *Studies In Logical Theory*.

[1] See Dewey's statement concerning this influence in Adams and Montague, editors, *Contemporary American Philosophy* (New York: Russell and Russell, Inc., 1962). Originally published in 1930.

[2] I have elaborated this position in "Two Views of the Nature of Knowledge," *Tulane Studies in Philosophy*, Vol. XVIII, 1969 pp. 85–91.

[3] Bridgman's *The Logic Of Modern Physics* had recently been published as Dewey wrote. See QC 111, note.

the solution of the original problem? The search for adequate responses and for ways of modifying the original data by reference to these responses is the process of inquiry. Knowledge arises from inquiry, and when the problem is solved knowledge has been achieved. The data by themselves are inchoate and lack meaning except as they are related in the process of inquiry to other data, especially those of memory and anticipation. It is only as the data enter into these relations that they take on meaning, and it is only as they take on meaning that they become the material of knowledge.

Dewey did not explicitly emphasize that his theory of knowledge depends on a behavioral theory of meaning but he insisted that the data of experience take on meaning by reference to their consequences, and that knowledge emerges from this context. I shall argue that the behavioral theory of meaning is fundamental to Dewey's major interests both in the philosophy of knowledge and the philosophy of value, even though he did not explicitly emphasize it. I have argued elsewhere that a behavioral theory of meaning is basic to a viable pragmatic philosophy and that the pragmatic theory of knowledge in general rests upon it.[1]

Dewey did not use the word "behavioral" in the 1920's; that came later. He did note only two years after the publication of Watson's *Behaviorism* that all of the *Essays In Experimental Logic* had been "written from the standpoint of what is now termed a behavioristic psychology" (EEL Prefatory Note). He recognized throughout that meanings are imported into experience by the behavior of human organisms.

II

The data of experience that pose the problem for inquiry are events, not objects. Events are relatively unformed and indefinite compared to objects. It is true that objects with meanings seem to be immediately present in *adult* perception (EN 318), but an object with a meaning is a product of past inquiries,

---

[1] See my article "Pragmatism and a Behavioral Theory of Meaning" in the title *Pragmatism Reconsidered* soon to be published in the "Monist Library of Philosophy" (La Salle, Ill., Open Court Publishing Company).

past responses, and communication within a social context. Ways of responding to events produce habits of action, and when these habits are called up "Events turn into objects, things with a meaning" (EN 166). By the help of language "They may be referred to when they do not exist, and thus be operative among things distant in space and time" (EN 166). Meanings are tools in solving the problems posed by inchoate events, not only the problems of the individual organism but those involving others, for human organisms depend on each other for survival, and common problems and common responses induce communication wherein words become symbols of meanings. Meanings are the definite relationships that can be established between events, reactions, and consequences. Reactions to events produce consequences, and "meaning is awareness of these consequences before they actually occur" (EN 324).

Two points are of importance here: first, the awareness of consequences and the ability to anticipate them are due to past inquiry and to what might be called induction from past instances though Dewey does not elaborate a theory of induction in connection with his discussion of events and objects.[1] But definite anticipations based on habits developed from successful dealing with past experiences are contributory to meanings. "In the degree in which reactions are inchoate and unformed, 'this' [the data of experience] tends to be the buzzing, blooming confusion of which James wrote. As habits form, action is stereotyped into a fairly constant series of acts having a common end in view" (QC 238).

The second of the two points remarked in the paragraph above is that the emergence of meaning takes place in the context of communication – a social context. Dewey's emphasis on the social context is an important part of his evolutionary naturalism. He brings this out in the first few paragraphs of his chapter on communication and meaning in *Experience and Nature*. The ability to grasp meaning is not an innate

---

[1] The chapter on induction in Dewey's *Logic: The Theory Of Inquiry*, Ch. XXI, criticizes the Aristotelian theory and advances Dewey's own theory in the context of scientific method. *Logic: The Theory Of Inquiry* (New York: Henry Holt and Company, 1938) will hereinafter be cited L with page number.

faculty of a substantial mind but rather is an evolutionary development of organisms in contact with each other subject to a shared environment and shared problems and dependent on cooperation for survival. Language is the establishment of communication for such cooperation (EN 179). Things acquire significance as they make possible shared cooperation (EN 180). A sound, gesture or written mark becomes language only in so far as it gains meaning "and it gains meaning when its use establishes a genuine community of action" (EN 185).

Meanings are not psychical to Dewey in any way in which "psychical" is opposed to "physical "or "natural." Meanings arise from tendencies of the organism to react to the relationship between present data and whatever in memory and anticipation the data call up ideationally, but what is ideational always goes back to behavioral criteria – to the possibilities of action and response. "Ideas are anticipatory plans and designs" (QC 166–7). Mind is not an entity according to Dewey's theory. There is no separate mind with a faculty of thought. Mind is what occurs in the process of experimental inquiry. It is reasonable to regard mind in this way just as we "frame ideas of stars, acids, and digestive tissues in terms of *their* behavior" (QC 229, Dewey's italics). It would be more nearly correct to say that mind is the process of thinking than that thinking is a product of mind. "Thought is not a property of something termed intellect" (QC 166). Dewey notes with approval (although also with some qualification) that thinking has been called deferred action. He prefers to call it "response to the doubtful as such" (QC 223–4).

In his article on "The Concept of the Reflex Arc" of 1896, Dewey points out that what impinges on receptor nerves is not a stimulus except in the light of a possible response.[1] The response gives the neural disturbance meaning as a stimulus. In an exactly parallel fashion, the consequences of every act give meaning to the data of experience which, when the act is performed, become the object calling it forth. Experience as *had* is not doubtful, but what it *means* is doubtful. Meaning is the relationship between what is immediately experienced and

[1] See Allen K. Smith, "Dewey's Transition Piece: The *Reflex Arc* Paper" in the present volume of *Tulane Studies in Philosophy*.

the connections and references both in action and as a result of action that ensue. The meaning refers to future possible experiences. Meaning is "position and relationship in an experience yet to be secured" (EEL 139).

Meanings are objective. Presently experienced data are, for all adult perception, embedded in a context. They take on aspects adhering to them by reason of this context, the context of possible response. Events occur; that is not in question. Something takes place and the question is, *exactly what* is it? The question can be answered only in the light of possible responses, and when seen in this light, what happens takes on meaning and becomes an object. Meanings are absorbed into what has become more adequate, richer and fuller data. "When an event has meaning, its potential consequences become its integral and funded feature" (EN 182). The presently experienced data display aspects belonging to them by reason of the ideational (behavioral) factors surrounding them. "Meaning is not indeed a psychic existence; it is primarily a property of behavior, and secondarily a property of objects" (EN 179). Data acquire meanings by becoming objects of cooperative acts. Because the responses of different human organisms are relevant to each others' survival and are shared, meanings are inherently communicable, that is, objective.

The meanings with which I have been concerned above have been empirical because all meaning starts from experience and is applied to experience. Dewey advances, however, and adequately extends his behavioral theory of meaning to mathematics. It is true that he says that mathematical relations "are meanings without direct reference to human behavior" (EN 192), but the emphasis here must lie on the word "direct." Although mathematical meanings originally arose by abstracting from such concrete situations as counting, measuring, and exchanging goods, they became independent of their concrete origins by becoming symbolic operations "performed exclusively with reference to facilitating and directing other operations *also symbolic in nature*" (QC 154, Dewey's italics). Abstractions of this sort and their symbolic representations make possible a system of concepts related to each other only as concepts, and this is what we find both in mathematics and in formal logic. Mathematics and formal logic are sciences wherein concepts are related to each other rather than to things and objects. If mathematics and formal logic are used to refer to experience, they refer only to possibilities of connection of *whatever* it is that is to be connected. Leaving out the specification of what is to be connected is part of the abstraction of the mathematical or logical system. But the abstract concepts of the system can be manipulated only in terms of symbols (L 395). The only existential consideration necessary to mathematics is the notation of the symbolism (L 396). "The result is not simply a higher degree of abstractness, but a new order of abstractions" (L 396).

A passage in *The Quest For Certainty* (156) adversely criticizes traditional English empiricism for not being able to account for mathematical ideas in its scheme. Several pages follow in which Dewey goes into detail to show the application of his own theory both to the history and to the procedures of mathematics. Numbers are neither essences nor properties of things in existence but are "designations of potential operations" (QC 159).

III

One of the characterizing features of American pragmatism considered as a movement in philosophy is its refusal to dichotomize experience into existences and values, or facts and values. The characteristic pragmatic position is that existences or facts cannot be separated from values. Existences and values can be distinguished for analytical purposes but they are not separate. Dewey seems to go farther than this and to hold that the difference between facts and values is largely a matter of emphasis.[1] He defines values in much the same terms as those in which he defines meanings, but there is a difference too. All values arise from the interaction between the data of experience, human responses, and consequences the same as do meanings; the difference is that values also involve enjoyment. When the complex situation in which meanings arise is enjoyed,

---

[1] John Dewey, *Art As Experience* (New York: Minton, Balch & Company, 1934), p. 15. Hereinafter cited AE with page number.

there is value (QC 259). Actually, however, the process of selection-rejection that carves objects out of events is the same process that is at the bottom of enjoyment.

In his later writings on value, Dewey tended to use the words "satisfaction" or "fulfillment" instead of "enjoyment" and when he did so "satisfaction" was not the name of a feeling but was a synonym of "fulfillment." In both *The Quest For Certainty* and *Art As Experience*, Dewey used "enjoyment" freely (QC 259, AE 27) without any phobia of the affective connotation of "enjoyment" that he later showed, especially in his paper "The Field of Value" written years later for the volume *Value: A Cooperative Inquiry*.[1] No matter whether feelings are allowed or disallowed as necessary factors in the experience of value, however, it is clear that values are produced by valuation in a way similar to that in which knowledge is produced by inquiry, and the two processes have much in common.

The qualitative aspect of experience is the esthetic aspect, but Dewey is not inclined to attribute *esthetic value* to it until it is taken up into objects and acts (AE 4); in other words, until it becomes part of the same transaction as that from which meanings emerge. A tension is set up between the esthetic aspect of experience and the consequent aspect, for the esthetic aspect is consummatory – attention rests in qualitative experience; but the conditions of life – the need for adjustment – draw attention away from immediate qualities to consequences. It is this tension that poses the problem for inquiry (QC 236,) and in the solution of the problem both knowledge and values emerge. The knowledge is an intellectual value, and there also may be esthetic and moral values according to the nature of the problem and the relative emphasis placed on qualities or consequences. If satisfaction is found in the object because of its individuality, its consummatory nature, and not because of its consequences or its use, the value is primarily esthetic;" ... delightfully enhanced perception or esthetic appreciation is of the same nature as enjoyment of any object that is consummatory" (EN 389). But the consequences even of intrinsic

[3] Ray Lepley, editor, *Value: A Cooperative Inquiry* (New York: Columbia University Press 1949). Hereinafter cited VCI with page number.

values cannot be escaped and should not be overlooked. All experience into which alternative possibilities of action enter makes up the field of moral valuation.[1] There is a consummatory aspect of all experience, but the consummations have consequences as well.

Because meanings arise when the qualitative aspect of experience gives rise to consequences and is regarded as a sign of these consequences, there is an intellectual factor in all valuation (AE 15–16). Dewey maintained this view right up to his latest writings on value. Valuation is "affective-ideational-motor behavior."[2] He says that if he were to sum up his moral generalizations in a categorical imperative, it would be "So act as to increase the meaning of present experience" (HNC 283). It is evident from his behavioral theory of meaning that this maxim, in effect, admonishes each person to make his experience a larger, richer, fuller, more adequate way of meeting and dealing with the course of events that constitute his world.

In his later writings, Dewey repudiated the concept of intrinsic value, and this was primarily because all experience has consequences. He never had liked the word "intrinsic" but he allowed for what other people used the word to denote. For example, "every experience is esthetic in as far as it is final or arouses no search for any other experience" (QC 235). All through his pragmatic philosophy, Dewey had refused to separate means and ends. This refusal is especially evident throughout *Human Nature and Conduct*. The only effective end is an "end-in-view" which when attained marks only a change in the direction of activity and becomes a new starting point. There are ends-in-view and there are also consummations or immediate enjoyments, "But to pass from immediacy of enjoyment to something called 'intrinsic value' is a leap for which there is no ground" (TV 41). Dewey's rejection of the concept of intrinsic value can be attributed, however, to an absolutistic

---

[1] John Dewey, *Human Nature And Conduct* (New York: The Modern Library, 1930), p. 278. First published in 1922. Hereinafter cited HNC with page number.
[2] John Dewey, *Theory Of Valuation* in *International Encyclopedia Of Unified Science*, Vol. II, No. 4 (Chicago: The University of Chicago Press, 1939). p. 52. Hereinafter cited TV with page number. See also TV 55. and 65, VCI 74.

interpretation of "intrinsic" and Dewey's rejection of any sort of absolutism (VCI 69).

Dewey later also tended to disallow or at least to de-emphasize the affective component in the behavior giving rise to values and to emphasize more heavily the conative component. He speaks of caring for or nurturing or prizing, but his exposition brings out the conative aspects of these activities (VCI 67). It is possible within the terms of Dewey's theory to define the affective aspects behaviorally, and I think that there is no occasion to down-grade them (VCI 147). Comparison of the two points of view might be enhanced if it is pointed out that Dewey's "caring" is "caring for" while I think "caring about" to be germane. But I agree with Dewey that in so far as feeling is wholly private, it does not enter into the statement of the theory. The disagreement here is probably on the application of the term "wholly private." Contrary to Dewey, I hold that what is *wholly* private *cannot* be communicated. No warning that it *should not* is necessary. Dewey's analysis of communication in Chapter V of *Experience and Nature* is much more adequate than is the analysis (or lack of it) upon which his doctrine of page 67 of *Value: A Cooperative Inquiry* is based.

The relation between esthetic value and moral value is clear in Dewey's theory but is not elaborated. The relation between esthetic value and artistic value in *Art As Experience* is not as clear but is elaborated at great length. My estimation of Dewey's difficulty here is that it stems from his emphasis on intellection in regard to both value and art. I agree that the intellect is an inseparable part of adult life, but it need not enter into esthetic experience or the experience of art in the rather obvious way in which Dewey insists. My own interpretation of Dewey here is that at bottom his theory of art is partly moral and partly esthetic, but since his esthetic theory is a moral theory of esthetic, this leaves Dewey's record as a moralist unblemished. But morals deals with consequences and the place of intellectual activity in the foresight of consequences is greater and different from its place in consummatory activity.

Others hold an interpretation different from that expressed

above, and I will agree that Dewey's moralism is not of the common or garden variety. He was not a moralist in the sense of pursuing fixed ends or goals of conduct – the whole of *Human Nature and Conduct* argues against such moralism. His sort of moralism is more fundamental and can be illustrated by a passage from *Logic: The Theory of Inquiry.* "The point which is important is that formalistic logic provides no possible ground for deciding upon one practical policy rather than another, and none for following out the consequences of a policy when put into operation as a test for its validity" (L 510). The remark about the impotence of formalistic logic is sufficient refutation for Dewey. He says a few lines later: "There are those to whom this result will present itself as a *reductio ad absurdum* of the theory in question."

IV

I have presented an interpretation of Dewey's theory of meaning, but I should emphasize that it is only one interpretation, for Dewey's writings do not contain a theory of meaning worked out in systematic detail. It would be a great help to his expositors and critics if they did. Dewey talks a great deal about meanings but he often uses the word in an uncritical, common-sense fashion. He uses the term in many different ways but they are all ways which demand a behavioral theory if articulated systematically. He recognizes that meanings are fundamental to knowledge and he goes into great detail about knowledge. But often he has a tendency to blur or at least not clearly to develop distinctions, as if he held that because nothing is absolutely separable from anything else everything must be mixed up with everything else. There is some danger that the quotations I have presented above in an attempt to explicate his usage make it sound clearer than it is because of their selection and brief compass.

Dewey's whole philosophy would have been clearer and more persuasive if he had made a systematic analysis of meaning. The most helpful elaboration would have been in the context of semiotic. From early to late he drops hints that meanings are carried by signs (ID 88, 99, QC 297; L 51–57). But he does

not explicate in systematic detail the nature and characteristics of the sign relation. Signs, especially the symbols of
language, through their place in human behavior (that is,
through their dependence upon a context of memories and
anticipations) take on reference to future possible reactions
and possibilities of the consequences of reactions. This is their
meaning, and this behavioral meaning is fundamental both to
Dewey's theory of knowledge and his theory of value.

MEAD ON THE SELF AND MORAL SITUATIONS

JON S. MORAN

St. Ambrose College

One of G. H. Mead's most valuable contributions to pragmatism was his analysis of the self. Many of the themes developed by other pragmatic thinkers were completed by this view of selfhood. Such was the case in the field of ethics. Although both John Dewey and C. I. Lewis were more prominent moral philosophers, it was Mead who developed the means of showing the ultimate relevance of the self in moral problem solving.

In the following account of the historical significance of Mead's ethical views I will focus upon the function of the self in the context of morally problematic situations. In so doing I will show how Mead's view of selfhood is of aid in the analysis of a difficulty in Dewey's ethics. This difficulty consists in the ambiguity involved in Dewey's description of the relationship between a situation in which moral choice is required and the activity of inquiry used to make an intelligent decision.

H. S. Thayer refers to this problem in his comprehensive history of pragmatism. As Thayer indicates, the ideas of situation and of inquiry were used by Dewey to relate facts and values.[1] The inquiry uncovers and orders facts; but the initial problematic situation poses the question to which the facts must be relevant. Inquiry is "the matrix of relation"[2] between facts and values in that it is through inquiry that facts are discovered and ordered so that valuations can reach their termination. But the process of valuation is initiated in a problematic situation. The nature of the problem encountered

[1] See H. S. Thayer, *Meaning and Action: A Critical History of Pragmatism* (Indianapolis: The Bobbs-Merrill Co., 1968), 383–414.
[2] *Ibid.*, 390.

in the initial situation determines which facts are relevant to subsequent inquiry. An act is valuable when it solves the particular problem which has been encountered.

Because the problematic situation "provides the criterion and authenticity of moral judgment and action,"[1] Thayer maintains that "one would expect that it would occupy most attention in probative deliberations over [Dewey's] theory. In fact, however, this has not been the case."[2] Specifically Thayer believes that Dewey is unclear as to the meaning of the uniqueness and individuality of a problematic situation. These qualities do not appear to be empirically testable as are the other features of Dewey's view. Thayer then questions whether Dewey has in fact shown that there is *"one unique solution* or resolution for each doubtful situation."[3] If several solutions are possible, the ultimate choice among solutions "would seem to be purely free, spontaneous and willful."[4]

At issue is the extent to which moral questions are amenable to rational methods. By pointing to the individuality and uniqueness of moral situations a pragmatic theorist is able to criticize the notion of a pre-established moral order. He is able to maintain that each situation must be investigated on its own merits before one can decide how to act. Yet if one encounters radical individuality and uniqueness in each problematic situation, it is difficult to see how specific moral problems can be solved by the application of a public, objective methodology.

In this paper I will contend that Mead's analysis of the self and moral situations allows one to draw three essential conclusions. First, it is unnecessary to show that individuality and uniqueness are properties of morally problematic situations. The crucial characteristic of these situations is perceived novelty. Second, a consideration of the nature of the self enables one to grasp how the degree of arbitrariness in the formulation of moral decisions can be reduced. Finally, Thayer is correct in his assessment that, as interpreted by the prag-

---

[1] *Ibid.*, 410.
[2] *Ibid.*, 411.
[3] *Ibid.* (Thayer's italics).
[4] *Ibid.*

matists, moral choice involves a degree of arbitrariness. But it remains to be shown how any theory which respects the concreteness of situations could avoid admitting that some willfulness is present in all moral decisions.

I. Selfhood and Problematic Situations

Like Dewey, Mead rejected the notion of an absolute order of ultimate moral ends. He did so for several reasons. First, the notion of a pre-established moral order militates against the full use of intelligence in moral situations.[1] It encourages a simple classificatory type of thought that leads one to ignore the complexity of concrete contexts. Second, this classificatory thought often fails to locate the difficulty within the moral situation itself. (PBE, 93) Often the individual tends to locate the problem within himself rather than in the elements of the social environment. This tendency is contrary to Mead's interest in social reform. Finally, when concrete situations are actually analysed, it is impossible to discover a hierarchy of values that applies in each case.

Note that while the last mentioned reason may be construed as a statement of testable fact, the first reason is itself a value judgment. It says in effect that one should exercise as much intelligence as possible in making moral decisions. The second reason is a consequence of Mead's view of the intimate relation between self and situation and will be discussed below. Nevertheless it is apparent that Mead was intent upon doing more than merely describing what is involved in moral decisions. He was advocating a particular type of approach to moral problems. To understand his justification for this approach one must grasp the nature and function of the self in moral conduct.

In a problematic, moral situation the self is placed in question. One is aware of a conflict involving a number of values. Given the nature of the situation it appears to be impossible to give equal weight to all desired consequences.

---

[1] G. H. Mead, "The Philosophical Basis of Ethics," in *Selected Writings*, edited by Andrew J. Reck (Indianapolis: The Bobbs-Merrill Co., 1964), 90. Hereafter PBE.

This necessity of choosing among conflicting goods is an essential feature of situations calling for moral judgments. In order to arrive at an intelligent solution to this problem one must order the relevant values in such a way that some of them have priority over the others. How is the individual to do this?

One cannot solve the problem intelligently by simply adopting modes of behavior that are socially approved. Morality is not a matter of mere custom. In fact as Mead maintained, one's moral world "does not lie under a larger determining environment" (PBE, 84). To understand why this is the case one must understand the nature of a problematic situation. And to understand the nature of a problematic situation one must first gain some insight into the self.

The essential characteristic of a self is reflexiveness – the ability to be an object to oneself.[1] Reflexiveness is made possible by taking the attitude of the generalized other, i.e., the attitude of the social group of which one is (or wishes to be) a member. (The stipulation, "or wishes to be," is explained below as a function of increased generalization in the conception of the other). Mead maintained that language is the main instrument by which one is able to adopt this generalized, social attitude. Because the use of language involves the recognition of universalized, social meanings, linguistic usage is a means by which an individual constructs a self concept against the background of social attitudes.

The maintenance of an adequately defined concept of selfhood is a dialectical process involving two functional components: The "I" and the "me."[2] The "me" is the self as object, the conventional component of the self. By attending to and attempting to grasp the significance of the responses of others to one's own behavior one constructs a conception of the general attitudes taken by others toward oneself. The self which is conceived in the light of these attitudes – the

---

[1] For the most detailed account of Mead's view of the self, see G. H. Mead, *Mind, Self and Society; from the Standpoint of a Social Behaviorist*, edited, with an Introduction, by Charles W. Morris (Chicago: University of Chicago Press, 1934). Hereafter MSS.

[2] For a concise account of the "I" and the "me," see G. H. Mead, "The Social Self," in *Selected Writings*, 142–149. Hereafter SS.

attitudes that compose the generalized other – is the "me."

Two additional characteristics of the construction of the "me" are relevant to our investigation. First, the concept of the generalized other and thus of the "me" is constructed by the individual. Hence one cannot conclude that each individual's conception of the generalized other is identical with that of all other individuals in the same social group. Different individuals select different types of responses as relevant to themselves.

A second important feature of the generalized other is the generalization process itself. This other which at first may represent one's immediate family can eventually come to signify a more universal, social group. In particular situations it may represent the community of all rational men. Because action performed in terms of this rational other may not coincide with the accepted values of one's concrete, social group, such action can represent a criticism of the social group. One acts as an ideal self within the context of an imagined, ideal community. The inherent possibility of this type of action coupled with the fact that the individual constructs his conception of the generalized other makes it possible to free oneself from direct, social influence.

The innovative thought and creative activity involved in social criticism is possible because the self is more than a "me"; it is also an "I." The "I" is the source of the spontaneous, unpredictable elements in immediate behavior. While the "me" gives form to the self, one responds to the "me" as an "I." As a "me" one grasps the social significance of one's acts. But because one responds as an "I," conduct is never totally determined by social attitudes.

One's immediate action as an "I" is never directly present in experience. Rather one can recognize the presence of the "I" in one's remembrance of past acts. The responses of the "I" influence the social environment. This in turn can modify one's view of oneself as a "me." Thus social conduct is a matter of various selves modifying one another's conduct and in so doing altering the generalized other present in the conduct of each.

This activity is a specific example of the mutual transaction between an organism and an environment. The organism, to be sure, depends upon its physical environment for nourishment and growth. And the influence of the social environment upon human beings is in part responsible for the growth of the self. But, to Mead, the environment also depends upon the organism. This is true not only because the activity of the organism changes features of the environment, but also because the environment is selected by the sensitivities of the particular organism. The stimuli to which the organism responds exist as stimuli because the organism is prepared to respond to them (MSS, 128–129).

A similar relationship exists between a self and a social environment. One's social environment corresponds to those activities of others to which one is prepared to respond. These activities and responses are part of one's conception of the generalized other. But the individual who selects stimuli and accordingly constructs his own conduct is an active participant within the social context. The conflict between social influence and individual choice "disappears when we recognize that this control by the community over its members provides the material out of which reflective moral consciousness builds up its own situations, but cannot exist as a situation until the moral consciousness of the individual constructs it" (PBE, 84).

The constructive activity of the individual is most important in a problematic situation. A problematic situation can be noticed only by contrast with an accepted "world which is there."[1] A problem is identified as a problem because it is differentiated from the aspects of the world that are not doubtful. The unquestioned aspects – the world which is there – represent the objects of habitual or conventional responses. In terms of the self they are those things to which one is prepared to respond as a conventional "me." On the other hand a problem is a problem precisely because one does not know how to respond to certain features of the world in conventional ways. Such a situation calls for an inquiry so that action

---

[1] G. H. Mead, *The Philosophy of the Present*, edited, with an Introduction, by Arthur E. Murphy with prefatory remarks by John Dewey (LaSalle, Ill.: Open Court Publishing Co., 1932), 5.

will be able to continue. When successful, this restructuring activity will eliminate the problematic character of a situation.

The interplay between creativity and convention in problem solving can be characterized in terms of the private and public aspects of behavior.[1] Let us take the creative scientist as an example. The scientist is confronted with a situation requiring a novel solution. He may notice that an experimental result contradicts established theory. The creative activity generating a new hypothesis is the work of the "I." It is a private activity in the sense that there is no generally accepted solution to the problem of which the scientist is aware. But once the hypothesis is generated it must be tested by public methods of inquiry. Thus the creative process is private, but the results are public to the extent that they can be tested by public methods. If they cannot be so tested, then the scientist must conclude that the hypothesis is inadequate.

Mead maintained that a moral solution to a problem is analogous to a scientific solution. However there is an important difference. Whereas a scientific solution may deal with abstracted, formal aspects of the world, a moral solution involves "concrete personal interests, in which the whole self is reconstructed in its relations to other selves whose relations are essential to its personality" (SS, 149). To illustrate this I will return to the description of the nature of a moral problem which began this section.

Before a moral problem arises a person functions habitually as a "me". We might say that his actions are in line with his character. But when a moral problem arises, the organization of the self undergoes a process of disintegration. One becomes aware of conflicting tendencies to act, of conflicting values. A motive for action is absent. The old self or "me" is placed in question; its assumptions are challenged.

If one merely attempts to reassert the claims of the old self, the problem is addressed in a subjective manner. One is conscious of the conflict as taking place between one's own subjective wishes and the subjective wishes of other selves who represent the tendencies and interests lacking in

[1] See G. H. Mead, "Scientific Method and Individual Thinker," in *Selected Writings*, 171–211.

the old self (SS, 148). If one reasserts one's old self, growth is stunted. And the true nature of the problem at hand is ignored. This situation is analogous to that of a scientist who, when confronted with novel experience, concludes that he needs new glasses.

A more profitable way of dealing with the problem is creatively to reconstruct the situation so that all relevant interests will be included in a motive for action. In so doing one acts as an "I." Attention is turned from the self as a "me" to the immediate situation. Alternative modes of conduct are considered and evaluated. The result includes both a reconstructed situation and a new self. Yet one is usually aware of the new situation before one is aware of the new self. This is so because the self as object appears in memory as an awareness of an attitude already formulated (SS, 148).

The creative approach to moral problems enables one to free oneself from the direct influences of acquired, social custom and of unregulated impulse. The previously socialized "me" is rejected when one refuses to allow the old self to dominate the situation. And unregulated impulses are restrained and guided by the reflective analysis of the situation.

At this point it is possible to answer the question concerning the empirical nature of the contention that moral situations are individual and unique. Remember that this contention is thought to be important, because its proponents are able to reject appeals to a pre-established moral order. A unique situation is unlike any other situation. If morally problematic situations are unique, solutions that apply in other situations are useless in the face of a presently confronted problem.

Theoretically the individuality and uniqueness of situations would result from the functioning of several factors. Both the environment and the inclinations of different selves contribute to the individuality of a particular situation. The moral agent individuates the situation by selecting stimuli to which he responds. But because one cannot select that which is absent, environmental elements also contribute to the uniqueness of a situation.

But can one empirically establish that any situation is radically unique or individual? To do so one would have to know how a situation differed from all other situations. This would seem to be beyond the experiential capabilities of any person. And it is absurd to assume that one would have to establish the presence of radical uniqueness in order to recognize a moral problem.

From the previous discussion of Mead's view of problematic situations, one can conclude that perceived novelty, not uniqueness, is the crucial characteristic. By "the perception of novelty" I mean that a self is aware that his customary responses to situations cannot be utilized in a situation presently encountered. Consciousness of novelty suffices to render a situation doubtful. It calls for the reconstruction of behavior and for the generation of new, hypothetical modes of response.

Before turning to Mead's view of the inquiry which should be used to deal with doubtful situations, one further point concerning novelty should be made. Perceived novelty, as described above, may not be one's immediate reaction to a morally problematic situation. At first one may not be clearly aware of the actual inappropriateness of customary responses. One may be merely confused. Some preliminary inquiry may be needed to clarify the real novelty of the situation. Nevertheless when novelty is apparent, one realizes that the problem at hand merits special consideration.

By shifting attention from radical individuality and uniqueness to novelty, I have eliminated only one of the difficulties apparently involved in a pragmatic approach to moral situations. A more important problem noted by Thayer is that which centers upon the relation between a morally problematic situation and the inquiry used to provide a solution to the perceived difficulty. Is there anything inherent in a moral situation that points to a specific solution to the problem encountered? Or is one finally forced to choose a mode of behavior in a willful and arbitrary manner? In order to answer these questions, I first must explain Mead's conception of the relevance of scientific methods to moral questions.

II. Obligation, Motives and the Scientific Method

Mead's advocacy of the scientific method as a means of inquiry into values was an attempt to avoid a divorce of values from facts. The public, scientific method impressed Mead as a pervasive aspect of correct thinking. This method is not, he said, "an agent foreign to the mind, that may be called in and dismissed at will."[1] Rather it is "an integral part of human intelligence and when it has once been set at work it can only be dismissed by dismissing the intelligence itself" (SM, 255). Thus moral decisions severed from rigorous application of scientific method would be forms of unintelligent behavior.

Nevertheless scientific method alone "does not undertake to say what the good is" (SM, 255). The values which guide one's conduct must be discovered in the process of living. But in problematic situations in which the relevance of values is unclear the scientific method serves to construct the situation in such a way that intelligent choices can be made.

What is required by the use of the method of science is the consideration of all conflicting values. These values must then be integrated to allow for intelligent conduct "with reference to all of them" (SM, 256). This is the case because the method is primarily "a highly developed form of impartial intelligence" (SM, 256).

The policy of action which Mead advocated is in conformity with Dewey's distinction between the desired and the desirable.[2] To state that which is desired or valued is merely to state a fact about a person – that he wants, or is inclined toward, certain things. This is not a value judgment. In a given situation one wants to know what *should* be desired. To answer this question one must consider all interests and desires, both one's own as well as those of other members of society.

The intimate relationship between scientific thought and

---

[1] G. H. Mead, "Scientific Method and the Moral Sciences," in *Selected Writings*, 255. Hereafter SM.

[2] John Dewey, *The Quest for Certainty* (New York: Minton, Balch & Co., 1929), 254–286.

moral choice is illustrated in Mead's account of the nature of the ideal, motives and obligation of moral behavior. The *ideal* pursued in moral conduct must be defined, Mead maintained, in terms of the "method of meeting the problem."[1] An attempt must be made to harmonize all values in such a manner that the problem ceases to exist. As noted above, it is impossible to define one's ideal in terms of a past value which guided nonproblematic conduct for it is precisely this old value which is challenged by the new situation. To force the new situation to fit the familiar mold may involve a refusal to face the situation. Nor can the ideal be defined in terms of the future situations to be created by one's action. One cannot presuppose what will be the ideal result of conduct before an inquiry is undertaken, for one cannot specify in detail what this future situation will be. There is no single, ideal end in all situations. But there is an ideal means of dealing with problems. This means involves the consideration of all values, factual details and future consequences that have a bearing on the situation in question.

The *motive* of moral conduct is intimately related to the nature of the ideal. The generalized motive of all moral choice should be the production of action which adequately harmonizes conflicting interests. The specific motive which guides one's conduct in a particular situation is a product of inquiry. This motive is not given in a problematic situation; it is created or constructed by the agent after possible alternatives are considered.

The motive is not a mere impulse. Impulses result in blind action. One impulse may conflict with another impulse. To act merely upon impulse is to risk the needless restriction of other impulses. Consequently the moral situation calls for a novel reconstruction of impulses to include them all within the eventual act. The resulting "tendency to action when brought into conscious relation with the other conflicting tendencies" (SPD, 22) is the motive of moral conduct in a particular situation. Rather than being an isolated impulse, the motive is found in the act of coordinating various impulses.

[1] G. H. Mead, "Suggestions Toward a Theory of the Philosophical Disciplines," in *Selected Writings*, 21. Hereafter SPD.

Finally moral *obligation* is located, not in an external, lawmaking power, but rather in the necessity of integrating oneself.

Obligation lies in the demand that all these values and impulses shall be recognized. The binding nature of obligation is found in the necessity for action, and in the claim made by the whole self for representation within the action; while the consequences of failure to meet the obligation are found in the sacrifice of certain parts of the self which carries with it the friction and sense of loss that is characteristic of the immoral attitude (SPD, 21).

One obligates oneself. Confronted with a conflict of values one is forced to act. But the choice of a particular line of behavior involves a risk. Moral decisions can be incorrectly made. The continued growth of selfhood can be interrupted or damaged. The self which one must become is a function, not only of one's biologically rooted aptitudes and impulses, but also of one's social situation. Failure to bring these factors into harmony has unfortunate consequences.

The necessity of weighing the consequences of certain impulses to act against the consequences of other impulses within the context of society links ethical and political behavior, individual choice and social reconstruction. The individual self develops from action toward, and reactions to, members of a society. One's self is social, because one measures one's actions against one's interpretation of the social context. And the conditions of action are also provided by society. The nature of the consequences of one's actions depends upon the reaction of others to one's conduct.

Consideration of one's social context lessens the tendency toward mere willfulness in the making of moral choices. The social context, the constellation of the interests of others, must be recognized as the existing field of future conduct. However the recognition of the interests of society allows for novel solutions to problems. It is possible for one to demand a change in social attitudes in order to create an atmosphere that is more congenial to the interests of all people.

The imperative n ature of moral judgments separates them

from other types of judgments resulting from inquiry. In predominantly factual inquiry predictions of states of affairs are made. But in moral inquiry more than factual prediction is involved. One *advocates* certain states of affairs. Specifically one advocates the adoption of attitudes on the part of others toward certain types of behavior. This advocacy of the social acceptance of various sorts of conduct involves a universal feature of moral thought (MSS, 379). This universality is most apparent in Mead's discussion of political rights.[1]

Mead pointed out that the idea of rights includes a process of generalization whereby rights must be understood as applying to all citizens. Specific rights are brought into the field of conscious discussion because particular social problems incline people to clarify their situation in order to solve the problems. Rights are legally recognized in order to avoid such problems. Laws or verbal agreements would have no real effect if they did not apply to all people in the same manner.

On the level of society, of civil laws and rights, the demand that one should recognize all competing interests is duplicated. This is a natural concomitant to individual, moral life. In weighing his decisions the individual must take into account the social consequences of his behavior. Because the actions of others have effects upon the consequences of one's own decisions, there will be a tendency to coordinate the desires of various individuals within the social fabric. When society must be readjusted in order to allow certain individuals to function within the society, moral decisions result in efforts to inaugurate social reform.

There is a relationship here between the social requirements of the development of selfhood and the social consequences of moral actions. An individual needs a social context in order to develop a self concept. As we have seen, the "me" results from taking the attitude of the generalized other. In the making of a moral decision the generalized other represents the social context, the coordinated group of social interests, in which the new "me" can find a place. Since

[1] G. H. Mead, "Natural Rights and the Theory of the Political Institution," in *Selected Writings*, 150–170.

the envisioned social environment at present may not exist, the actions of the individual help to create the new order. The social reform resulting from one's choice of goals is possible only if its incipient causes are present as potentialities in the existing society. Thus one must make an attempt to understand the possibilities of development in the present situation.

Although Mead denied that moral decisions must be mere imitations of a pre-existing model which society provides, society – as the totality of individuals responding to one another in similar ways – does provide certain favored roles which the individual is influenced to adopt. The influence of society upon the individual, although not total, is significant. Thus when Mead said that society provides the material for moral decisions, this included the idea that society provides the context and group of roles which an individual is pressured to adopt.

An understanding of the roles present in society can be gained from a study of the social sciences. The results of social inquiries may be included as data in one's moral inquiries. If one wishes to criticize traditional modes of behavior, one can do so by showing that the adoption of new forms of activity will benefit all members of society. In this manner a moral decision can be justified to others in the same way that it is justified to oneself. To justify one's behavior one must show that the consequences of one's actions harmonize the interests of individuals better than conventional actions. If the attempt at justification is successful, one advocates that others act in similar ways when confronted with similar situations. In this manner the social context acts as a guide in making moral decisions.

III. Novelty and Willfulness

In the first section of this paper I concluded that perceived novelty, rather than radical individuality or uniqueness, is the crucial character of morally problematic situations. For Mead the presence of novelty eliminates the possibility of merely deducing one's subsequent conduct from a set of absolute laws. Instead one must attempt to invent or discover a hypothetical plan of action which will do justice to the multifarious facets of a problematic situation.

The question which remains is whether or not there is a willful or arbitrary aspect to all moral decisions. It is clear that for Mead moral choice is not a matter of *mere caprice* as long as one employs the scientific method, including the ideal of considering all relevant interests. The scientific method is used to direct the otherwise purely willful and arbitrary results of impulsive inclinations. It does so by allowing one to construct a rational motive for action.

But is there only one rational motive in any specific situation? Can Mead contend that there is a single morally correct course of action in each instance? Because proposed courses of action are like scientific hypotheses, one can conceive of the possibility that different hypothetical modes of behavior could integrate the same constellation of interests. Different hypotheses may be tested by acting in accordance with their requirements and noting the consequences. Yet in regard to moral questions individuals may still differ as to the success of different hypotheses, because they differ in their estimation of the degree of emphasis to be placed upon different interests.

People may also disagree in their estimation of what constitutes a morally problematic situation. That which is a problem to one person may present no difficulty to another person. To the extent that individuals share a similar cultural background, differences in the determination of problems may be minimized. But we cannot expect that the differences will be totally eliminated.

Are we then to assume that solutions to moral problems are legitimate only to those individuals who feel that they are legitimate? Do the moral results of the scientific method ultimately depend, not upon any factors intrinsic to the method itself, but upon personal quirks? Is there no way of publicly justifying moral decisions?

Mead's response to questions such as these is not always clear, but the following answer can be constructed from the preceding account of Mead's ethics. First, one should not assume that all moral differences can be overcome. The elimination of an absolute, pre-established moral order eliminates the possibility of conclusive proof in moral matters. Proposed solutions can always be re-evaluated. Second, those questions which affect a large group of individuals – for example questions concerning fundamental political rights – and which are associated with the possibility of social upheaval, may be most likely to result in some sort of agreement by way of compromise.

Finally, an increased awareness of the nature of the social self may increase the possibilities of agreement. When one realizes that the generation and growth of selfhood is the result of a social process, one is more likely to see the importance of coordinating various interests in society. One is also more likely to acknowledge the link between problematic situations and social reform and to favor those proposals that entail positive social reconstruction.

Even when the social context is considered, however, the validity of moral judgments cannot be established with certainty. Yet Mead did not view this as a deficiency in his ethical theory. He contended that lack of finality or certainty are deficiencies only to those who maintain that ultimate solutions presently are available. Seeing no way of verifying the reality of a universal moral order, Mead, like Dewey, turned his attention to the discovery of means of dealing with moral problems in specific situations. In so doing he was primarily interested in showing how impulses or desires could be rationally channeled. He did not wish to advocate the elimination of impulses and desires as factors in moral conduct.

Whether one can do justice to the complexity of moral situations while defending an absolute moral code is a question which is yet to be answered. This problem has been recognized by moral theorists other than the pragmatists. Often Mead was unfair in his assessment of the myopia of advocates of a pre-established moral order. Yet his criticisms resulted from his distaste for moral principles divorced from the concrete activities of human selves. And his contextual analysis of moral situations gave testimony to his belief that ignorance of the complexity of existing circumstances is too high a price to pay for comforting, but artificial, clarity.

EPISTEMOLOGY IN WILLIAM JAMES'S
PRINCIPLES OF PSYCHOLOGY

ANDREW J. RECK

Tulane University

I. Introduction

Among classic American philosophers William James ranks after John Dewey as a contributor to the philosophy of education.[1] It is fitting that a collection of essays in honor of Professor George Barton, who has devoted his intellectual energies to the philosophy of education as well as to social and political philosophy and to the history of recent philosophy, should contain an essay on James. Since, on a previous occasion, I have, at the instance of an invitation from Professor Barton, participated in a symposium centering on James's educational theory,[2] I propose here to investigate a topic in his *Principles of Psychology* – namely, the epistemology to be found in that work.

Certainly James considered psychology to be fundamental to educational theory, as his talks to teachers make plain. He stipulated that the chief professional task of the teacher consists "in training the pupil to behavior" (TT, 28), and he defined education as "the organization of acquired habits of conduct and tendencies to behavior" (TT, 29). Thus James's conception of education seems to depart from such traditional theories as Plato's, for which education and knowledge are necessarily connected in the sense that the end of the former

[1] See William James, *Talks to Teachers on Psychology and to Students on Some of Life's Ideals* (London & New York: Longmans Green & Co., 1899). Hereafter this work will be cited in parentheses in the text by the abbreviation "TT" followed by the page number.

[2] Plenary Session, chaired by Kenneth Benne, with Elisabeth Flower as speaker on "The Inquiries of William James," and George E. Axtelle, Andrew Reck, and Robert Schwartz as participants, at the 23rd Annual Meeting of the Philosophy of Education Society, in New Orleans, Louisiana, on March 22, 1967. The session was taped.

is the latter. But in the light of James's pragmatism, the differences between knowledge and behavior which traditional theories underscore are reduced, so that behavior as the end of education is tantamount to knowledge. James's theory of knowledge, his epistemology, then, is basic for his educational theory.

The present paper will examine James's epistemology as it unfolds in the *Principles*. No attempt will be made to deal with the later writings in which James expounded his pragmatism and his radical empiricism. The restriction of the investigation to the *Principles* leaves no small task. After all, the *Principles of Psychology* is widely regarded as James's greatest work, and epistemological discussions cover many pages of this work. James's later and more popular epistemological writings may perhaps be best understood after an understanding of his epistemology in the *Principles*. Yet, despite the voluminous and growing literature on James's thought, the epistemology in the *Principles* is a relatively neglected topic, overshadowed by the later doctrines.

II. *"Erkenntnistheorie"*

In the *Principles* James used the term *Erkenntnistheorie* to denote epistemology. Although James used the German word by preference, he wanted no part of the German thought. *Erkenntnistheorie* in nineteenth century post-Kantian German philosophy had a meaning wholly at odds with James's conception of knowledge. Now James's basic intention in the *Principles* is to establish psychology as a natural science.[1] Consequently, he was devastatingly critical of the Kantian transcendental psychology, while the scientific point of view he adopted in psychology radically affected the theory of knowledge. As James wrote:

In German philosophy since Kant the word *Erkenntnistheorie*, criticism of the faculty of knowledge, plays a great part. Now the psychologist necessarily becomes such an *Erkenntnistheoretiker*. But the knowledge he theorizes about is not the bare function of know-

[1] See Andrew J. Reck, "The Philosophical Psychology of William James," *The Southern Journal of Philosophy*, Vol. 9 (1971), 293–312.

ledge which Kant criticises – he does not inquire into the possibility of knowledge *überhaupt*. He assumes it to be possible, he does not doubt its presence in himself at the moment he speaks.[1]

Now in this passage James's transformation of epistemology is quite revolutionary, presaging twentieth century developments in the field. He has rejected the traditional problem of justifying knowledge, and has turned instead to the problems of criticism and analysis. But the context in which James introduced his epistemological revolution mingles common sense and science, as his own words reveal: "The knowledge he [the psychologist] criticises is the knowledge of particular men about the particular things that surround them. This he may, upon occasion, in the light of his *own* unquestioned knowledge, pronounce true or false, and trace the reasons by which it has become one or the other" (PP, I, 184).

James's dismissal of *Erkenntnistheorie* as it was presented by the post-Kantians is twofold. First, James rejected it because it concentrates on questions which, given the terms in which they are framed, are inherently unanswerable. An implication of this line of argument is the positivist repudiation of metaphysics. Second, James excluded *Erkenntnistheorie* from psychology as a science because, like other sciences, psychology need not trouble itself with epistemological questions, but may make assumptions concerning knowledge. The second line of argument is evident in the following sentence, in which, delineating the assumptions of the scientific psychologist, James said: "About such *ultimate* puzzles [as how the psychologist can know and report his object] he in the main need trouble himself no more than the geometer, the chemist, or the botanist do, who makes precisely the same assumptions as he" (P, I, 184). Sometimes, however, both lines of argument are compressed in the same passage as when James wrote:

... the *relation of knowing* is the most mysterious thing in the world. If we ask how one thing *can* know another we are led into the heart of *Erkenntnistheorie* and metaphysics. The psychologist, for his part,

---

[1] William James, *The Principles of Psychology* (New York: Holt, 1890), I, p. 184. Hereafter this work will be cited in parentheses in the text by the abbreviation "P" followed by the volume and page number.

does not consider the matter so curiously as this ... Knowledge becomes for him an ultimate relation that must be admitted, whether it be explained or not ... (PP, I, 216).

Now prima facie the first line of argument is critical, the second uncritical. The first discloses that the basis of traditional *Erkenntnistheorie* is chimerical. The second disregards epistemological questions on the grounds that they are irrelevant to scientific psychology, and recommends proceeding on assumptions adopted uncritically. It is assumed not only that knowledge exists, but also that knowledge is a relation. As James's discussion of knowledge unfolds in the *Principles*, however, it will become apparent that he developed, within the framework of psychology as a science, another critique of knowledge to replace the theories of the nineteenth century epistemologists.

III. Dualism

Besides assuming that knowledge exists, and that it is a relation, James also construed the cognitive relation dualistically. He declared: *"The psychologist's attitude toward cognition ... is a thoroughgoing dualism.* It supposes two elements, mind knowing and thing known, and treats them as irreducible" (P, I, 218). In an article published in the preceding volume of this journal,[1] I have shown how an unquestioned epistemological dualism dominated the *Principles*. Indeed, I have suggested that when James wrote the *Principles of Psychology* dualisms, psychophysical and epistemological, were so entrenched that he did not attempt to overcome them. I do not wish in the present paper to cover old ground, but in order to advance the discussion, some points will bear repeating.

It is helpful to recall that James's commitment to epistemological dualism was not simply an acquiescence in what was prevalent in nineteenth century philosophy. On the contrary, James seized upon epistemological dualism as a therapeutic instrument in the establishment of psychology as a science. It

---

[1] Andrew J. Reck, "Dualisms in William James's *Principles of Psychology*," *Tulane Studies in Philosophy*, XXI (1972), 23–38.

is the key to his detection of what he called "the psychologist's fallacy." This fallacy consists in the psychologist's *"confusion of his own standpoint with that of the mental fact* about which he is making his report" (P, I, 196). In other words, the idea the psychologist has in mind concerning the object he is investigating is erroneously equated with this object. The psychologist's fallacy collapses the relation between idea and object upheld by epistemological dualism. James cited as a glaring instance of this fallacy in nineteenth century psychology the theory that all consciousness is self-consciousness. The psychologist who advocates such a theory of "apperception" or "reflection" is misled by "the assumption that the mental state studied must be conscious of itself as the psychologist is conscious of it" (P, I, 197).

It is helpful also to recall how James formulated his epistemological dualism, placed as it is within his overarching theory of consciousness as a stream and a function. In the famous Chapter IX of the *Principles*, in which James portrayed consciousness as a stream of ideas and feelings which overlap, he underscored as the fourth characteristic of consciousness the fact that: *"Human thought appears to deal with objects independent of itself; that is, it is cognitive, or possesses the function of knowing"* (P, I, 271). Now this formula calls for analysis. It does not assert that objects exist independent of consciousness; but that in cognition consciousness *seems to deal* with such objects. The formula, then, is ontologically neutral. Nevertheless, James did attempt to clarify his concept of "object." His clarification poses a distinction between the "object" of thought and its "topic." Take the thought expressed by the sentence "Columbus discovered America in 1492." According to James,

... the *Object* ... is really its entire content for deliverance, neither more nor less. ... The object ... in the sentence, for example, is strictly speaking neither Columbus, nor America, nor its discovery. It is nothing short of the entire sentence, "Columbus-discovered-America-in-1492" (P, I, 275).

On this analysis the object of thought is no simple entity, but rather a complex almost without limit. By contrast, the "topic' of thought is a "fractional object." It is a selected or named "substantive kernel or nucleus of consciousness" (P, I, 275).

In James's account of cognitive consciousness in the *Principles*, the topic of thought, and not the object, occupies the central position. For in James's description of consciousness the fifth characteristic is that consciousness "... *is always interested more in one part of its object than another, and welcomes and rejects, or chooses, all the while it thinks*" (P, I, 284). Out of the objects of its thoughts consciousness selects its topics. The objects are compared to raw materials upon which the mind operates to create its works – i.e., topics. Ontology is replaced by a metaphysics of experience as the following passage reveals:

The mind, in short, works on the data it receives very much as a sculptor works on his block of stone. In a sense the statue stood there from eternity. But there were a thousand different ones beside it, and the sculptor alone is to thank for having extricated this one from the rest. Just so the world of each of us, howsoever different our views of it may be, all lay embedded in the primordial chaos of sensations, which gave the mere *matter* to the thought of all of us indifferently. We may, if we like, by our reasonings unwind things back to that black and jointless continuity of space and moving clouds of swarming atoms which science calls the only real world. But all the while the world *we* feel and live in will be that which our ancestors and we, by slowly cumulative strokes of choice, have extricated out of this, like sculptors, by simply rejecting portions of the given stuff. Other sculptors, other statues from the same stone! Other minds, other worlds from the same monotonous and inexpressive chaos! My world is but one in a million alike embedded, alike real to those who may abstract them. How different must be the worlds in the consciousness of ant, cuttle-fish, or crab! (P, I, 288–89).

Typically Jamesian in style, the quoted passage may well defy analysis. Opening with an illuminating analogy between a mind and a sculptor, it closes appealingly with a reference to an ant, cuttle-fish, or crab. And its originality is undeniable. Indeed, it introduces conceptions which later phenomenologists have elaborated into the doctrine of the *lebenswelt*. So far as these conceptions bear upon James's treatment of belief and of the perception of reality, they will be considered later in the present essay. In addition, the passage suggests ideas which belong to the metaphysics underlying the *Princi-ples*, a metaphysics which is not within our compass here. More pertinent is the epistemology the passage contains.

According to this epistemology, mind is active, but it is not all-creative. Given to it is a "chaos of sensations." The activity of mind in regard to this chaos is focussed in attention; it selects some materials from this chaos and rejects all other materials. What it selects becomes its topics, those partial objects which make up its knowledge and its reality. Thus the terms of James's epistemological dualism, despite its initially seeming to support a naively realistic ontology, are ultimately situated within an all-embracing experience beyond which knowledge does not reach.

The epistemology in the *Principles*, then, lends itself to the sort of formulation which is characteristic of James's later radical empiricism. Within the *Principles*, where James is bent on the establishment of psychology as a science, the formulation of his epistemology is cast in somewhat different language. Epistemology as the critique of knowledge falls wholly within the compass of psychology as a science, just as the terms of knowledge fall within experience.

James's revolution in epistemology is conspicuous in his resolution of the major problem for traditional epistemological dualism – namely, the incapacity of a mind to know that its thought knows its object, since there is no standpoint outside the mind to compare the thought with its object. Appreciation of James's treatment of the problem in the *Principles* may be enhanced by his estimation of Royce's solution of the problem along monistic lines in *The Religious Aspect of Philo-sophy* (1885). In a letter to Renouvier dated March 29, 1888, James called Royce's argument "irresistible, so long as we take the relation of really *intending* an object, *au sérieux*."[1] In the same letter he offered a brief elucidation of Royce's argument.

... a thought can be *of* something else, if it be *used* by some power which owns both it and the object, and *applies* one to the other,

[1] Ralph Barton Perry, *The Thought and Character of William James* (Boston: Little, Brown and Company, 1935), I, p. 705. Hereafter this work will be cited in parentheses in the text by means of the abbreviation *TCWJ* followed by volume and page numbers.

meaning that the thought *shall stand* for the object. *Then,* of course, the thought can represent, either rightly or wrongly, the object which it stands for. Otherwise there can be no question of error or truth (TCWJ, I, 704).

For Royce, therefore, truth and error depend upon the positing of some power, the Absolute Mind, transcending all finite minds, embracing them and the objects of their thoughts, and comparing the ideas of these minds with the objects of these ideas.

It is ironic that, despite James's suspicion that Royce's argument was inconclusive, he did not feel that he had overthrown this argument, as Ralph Barton Perry reports, until "1893 or thereabouts" (TCWJ, I, 799). It is ironic because in 1890 in the *Principles* James sketched an epistemology which explains how an idea can be known to correspond or fail to correspond to its object in the terms of a naturalistic psychology alternative to Royce's idealistic monism. Declaring that no explanation is forthcoming so long as the mind that knows is considered to be Absolute since there is no standpoint outside such a mind which allows the comparison of its ideas with its objects, James substituted the mind of the scientific psychologist for the Absolute.

James's resolution of the major problem of traditional epistemological dualism is ingenious. After all, the scientific psychologist studies minds – finite minds as they exist in nature. He studies their ideas, and he also has access to the objects of their ideas. Hence the psychologist himself, according to James, "...can go bail for the independent reality of the objects of which they think. He knows these to exist outside as well as inside the minds in question; he thus knows whether the minds think and *know*, or only think..." (P, I, 217). Thus for James the scientific psychologist becomes the master critic of knowledge, the epistemologist supreme.

Of course the psychologist as critic of knowledge employs tests "...to decide whether the state of mind he is studying is a bit of knowledge, or only a subjective fact not referring to anything outside itself" (P, I, 217). What are these tests? James's answer is that the psychologist "uses the tests we all practically use" (P, I, 217). In regard to a state of mind with cognitive value, the tests are threefold: (1) the idea in question resembles the psychologist's idea of the same reality, or (2) "...without resembling his idea..., it seems to imply that reality and refer to it by operating upon it through the bodily organs," or (3) "...it resembles and operates on some other reality that implies, and leads up to, and terminates in, the first one..." (P, I, 217). A state of mind lacks cognitive worth when, despite its resemblance to a reality or set of realities as known by the psychologist, it altogether fails "to operate on them or modify their course by producing bodily motions which the psychologist sees..." (P, I, 217). Thus there are two criteria to mark off the true from the false: (1) resemblance and (2) bodily motions affecting the course of reality.

On James's analysis resemblance is a complex relation. It is at once a relation between two ideas, one in the mind studied and one in the psychologist's mind, a relation between the idea in the mind studied by the psychologist and the reality the psychologist sees, and a relation between the psychologist's idea and reality. It is remarkable how, perhaps as a result of Royce's influence, James's account of resemblance approximates the scholastic theory of truth. Whereas, for example, according to St. Thomas Aquinas an idea is true if it agrees with reality and also with the idea in the mind of God, for James an idea is true if it agrees with reality and also with the idea in the mind of the psychologist who, almost like the Thomistic God, apprehends the first idea and also sees the reality to which it refers. The difference between the Thomistic doctrine and James's theory should not be missed, however. For St. Thomas even the reality is said to be true so far as it agrees with the idea in the mind of God, while for James the psychologist's idea is true only if it agrees with reality.

Moreover, in an anticipation of pragmatism, James appealed to a behavioral criterion of truth. Examining dream phenomena with factual coincidence, such as the case in which one dreams of the death of a certain man and the man dies, James denied that the dream has cognitive worth merely because of its agreement with a fact. Rather James regarded the dream as a sheer coincidence unless "the Subject were constantly having such dreams, all equally perfect, and...on awaking he had a habit of acting immediately as if they were true and so getting 'the start' of his more tardily informed neighbors ... And whatever doubts any one preserved would completely vanish if it should appear that from the midst of his dream he had the power of *interfering* with the course of the reality, and making the events in it turn this way or that, according as he dreamed they should" (P, I, 218). Hence, in this foreshadowing of pragmatism, the inert relation of resemblance is superseded by behavioral effectiveness as a criterion of truth.

IV. Knowledge of Acquaintance and Knowledge-about

The critic of knowledge examines an idea or a judgment for its cognitive worth by means of another idea or judgment which comprehends both the first idea or judgment and its object. The process of criticism, proceeding from one idea to the next, could in principle continue without end. But, in fact, belief, and not critique, is the characteristic state of cognitive consciousness. Later we shall return to James's theory of belief. Here it will suffice to note that belief as a matter of psychological fact brings all criticism to a terminus. But the question arises: Is there an epistemological justification for the termination of the process of critique? Or, in other words, is there a definite, accessible bedrock for all knowledge which, when reached, terminates critique? James seems to have offered such a justification, such a bedrock, when, citing John Grote and Herman Helmholtz, he introduced an important distinction between two kinds of knowledge: knowledge of acquaintance and knowledge-about (P, I, 221).[1] Let us briefly review differences James stressed between the two.

---

[1] John Grote, *Exploratio Philosophica* (Cambridge and London: Deighton, Bell. and Co., and Bell and Daldy, 1865), p. 60. H. Helmholtz, *Popular Lectures on Scientific Subjects*, trans. by E. Atkinson (London: Longmans, Green, and Co., 1873), pp. 308–309. For a discussion of the literature pertinent to this distinction, a discussion aimed mainly at establishing Grote as its originator, see Lauchlin D. Mac Donald, *John Grote, a Critical Estimate of his Writings* (The Hague: Martinus Nijhoff, 1966), pp. 235–241. A simular but unnoticed distinction was drawn by Shadworth Hodgson in his book, *Time and Space* (London: Longmans, Green, 1865). Hodgson distinguished between first intentions and second intentions, the

First, knowledge of acquaintance has to do with the simple natures of things, whereas knowledge-about pertains to their inner nature and also to the mesh of their relations to other things. As James said, "All the elementary natures of the world, its highest genera, the simple qualities of matter and mind, together with the kinds of relation that subsist between them, must either not be known at all, or known in this dumb way of acquaintance without *knowledge-about*" (P, I, 221). Simple qualities, relations, and classes, then, are the objects of knowledge of acquaintance. In some respects they are similar to what in post-Jamesian epistemologies came to be known as sense-data and essences, but the similarity cannot be pressed too far. James was articulating an original distinction, but he did not have at hand the analytic concepts and the logical tools he needed.

Second, knowledge of acquaintance is immediate or intuitive, it arises in direct experience devoid of analysis. James reserved the term "feeling" for states of consciousness in which knowledge of acquaintance occurs, and the term "feeling" applies to "the *emotions*, and the *sensations* we get from skin, muscle, viscus, eye, ear, nose, and palate" (P, I, 222). Knowledge-about involves analysis, especially of a thing in its relations to other things. James reserved the term "thought" (including "conceptions" and "judgments") to refer to knowledge-about. James's elucidation of this difference is worthy of quotation:

We can relapse at will into a mere condition of acquaintance with an object by scattering our attention and staring at it in a vacuous trance-like way. We can ascend to knowledge *about* it by rallying our wits and proceeding to notice and analyze and think. What we are only acquainted with is only *present* to our minds; we *have* it, or the idea of it. But when we know about it, we do more than merely have it; we seem, as we think over its relations, to subject it to a sort of *treatment* and to *operate* upon it with our thought. The words *feeling* and *thought* give voice to the antithesis. Through feelings we become acquainted with things, but only by our thoughts do we know about them. Feelings are the germ and starting point of cognition, thoughts the developed tree (P, I, 222).

former corresponding to knowledge by acquaintance and the latter to knowledge-about. In at least one passage of the *Principles* James, in referring to the distinction, reverted to Hodgson's language (P, II, 4).

Third, language provides means for expressing knowledge-about, and in fact knowledge-about may always be expressed in language. Hence wherever there is language, there is some degree of knowledge-about. On the other hand, knowledge of acquaintance is ineffable. There is no way of describing an object of knowledge of acquaintance. As James said:

I am acquainted with many people and things, which I know very little about, except their presence in the places where I have met them. I know the color blue when I see it, and the flavor of a pear when I taste it; I know an inch when I move my finger through it; a second time, when I feel it pass; an effort of attention when I make it; a difference between two things when I notice it; but *about* the inner nature of these facts or what makes them what they are, I can say nothing at all. I cannot *describe* them, make a blind man guess what blue is like, define to a child a syllogism, or tell a philosopher in just what respect distance is just what it is, and differs from other forms of relation. At most, I can say to my friends, Go to certain places and act in certain ways, and these objects will probably come (P, I, 221).

This does not mean for James that knowledge of acquaintance is never linked to language. Rather it may be represented by the grammatical subject in a sentence, provided there is little content in the subject-concept. As James said, it "must be named by the word that says the least. Such a word is the interjection, as *lo! there! ecco! voilà!* or the article or demonstrative pronoun introducing the sentence, as *the, it, that*" (P, I, 222).

Many languages, as James pointed out, signal the distinction between knowledge of acquaintance and knowledge-about by means of pairs of words for the English word "knowledge" – "thus, γνῶναι, εἰδέναι; noscere, scire; kennen, wissen; connaître, savoir" (P, I, 221). The distinction, moreover, may be taken to be epistemologically absolute. After all, knowledge of acquaintance is immediate or pre-reflective, ineffable or pre-predicative, had or felt; knowledge-about is the product of analysis and reflection, it is discursive, and it is thought. Undoubtedly, James's philosophy exhibits an empiricist emphasis which regards knowledge of acquaintance to be the bedrock of knowledge. The empiricist emphasis is paramount in those passages in which James appealed to "the prerogative position of sensations" in knowledge (P, II, 305). For sensations are had or felt, they are objects of knowledge of acquaintance, and knowledge-about, which involves concepts, derives its validity from the foundation of sensations upon which it rests. Although the empiricist emphasis is evident in James's *Principles of Psychology*, it pervades most thoroughly his later writings on radical empiricism. Nevertheless, it should be recognized that Bertrand Russell, and not William James, has been its leading advocate in the past century. As Russell declared: "Every proposition which we can understand must be composed wholly of constituents with which we are acquainted."[1] Still there is enough of an empiricist emphasis in James's thought to inspire the interpretation along the lines of constructional theory furnished by A. J. Ayer.[2]

For James, however, the empiricist emphasis, while present in his philosophy, does not dominate it. The distinction between knowledge of acquaintance and knowledge-about is not absolute, nor is the former the foundation of the latter. As James said,

> ... in general, the less we analyze a thing, and the fewer of its relations we perceive, the less we know about it and the more our familiarity with it is of the acquaintance-type. The two kinds of knowledge are, therefore, as the human mind practically exerts them, relative terms. That is, the same thought of a thing may be called knowledge-about it in comparison with a simpler thought, or acquaintance with it in comparison with a thought of it that is more articulate and explicit still (P, I, 221–222).

In affirming the relativity of the distinction between two kinds of knowledge, James participated in what is, in fact, the genuine revolution in epistemology in the past century. His contribution may well be called "the contextualist thesis."

---

[1] Bertrand Russell, "Knowledge by Acquaintance and Knowledge by Description," *Proceedings of the Aristotelian Society*, XI (1910–1911), 117; and *The Problems of Philosophy* (New York: Henry Holt & Co., 1911), p. 91.

[2] See A. J. Ayer, *The Origins of Pragmatism* (San Francisco: Freeman, Cooper and Company, 1968), Book II. Curiously James's distinction between two kinds of knowledge is slighted, being mentioned only in the comment on sensations and perceptions (217–218). This neglect is symptomatic of the manner in which commentators pass over the epistemology in the *Principles*.

Whereas the empiricist emphasis assumes that the traditional quest for an absolute basis for knowledge is valid, and proposes that knowledge of acquaintance terminates the quest, the contextualist thesis abandons the quest altogether, and leads instead to different bases for knowledge relative to the contexts in which thought seeks a basis.

V. Conception

One sort of reasoning behind James's epistemological revolution may be called, in accord with current usage, "phenomenological."[1] Mental acts take precedence over the objective contents of consciousness. Hence a subjective activity is what makes the difference between knowledge of acquaintance and knowledge-about. Having and feeling, on the one hand, and thinking, on the other hand, are indifferent in regard to their objects, capable of occurring in regard to any object, so that the same object may be felt or thought, depending wholly on the mind's activity. Although the phenomenological interpretation discards or ignores the scientific, experimental side of James's psychology, stressing instead a type of transcendental psychology in which the structure of the mind with its intentions is central, James's treatment of conception provides a degree of support for this interpretation.

James opened his discussion of conception in Chapter XII of the *Principles* with a consideration of the two kinds of knowledge. That there are possible two kinds of knowledge, he asserted, is due to "the principle of constancy in the mind's meanings" (P, I, 459). Called "the sense of sameness" and esteemed to be "the very keel and backbone of our thinking," this principle holds that "the mind can always intend, and know when it intends, to think of the Same" (P, I, 459). It pertains to the mind's structure and not to the universe. As James declared: "We are psychologizing, not philosophizing" (P, I, 459).

The principle of sameness is fundamental to all conceptual knowledge. For James defined conception as "the function by

---

[1] See Bruce Wilshire, *William James and Phenomenology: A Study of "The Principles of Psychology,"* (Bloomington: Indiana University Press, 1969).

which we ... identify a numerically distinct and permanent subject of discourse" (P, I, 461). The term "conception" denotes, to use James's words, "neither the mental state nor what the mental state signifies, but the relation between the two, namely, the *function* of the mental in signifying just that particular thing" (P, I, 461). When conception occurs, then, the flux of experience, the stream of consciousness, is arrested. For the mind selectively attends to a part of the flux; it fixes that part, excluding from it every other part. As James said: "Each conception thus eternally remains what it is, and never can become another ... Thus, amid the flux of opinions and of physical things, the world of conceptions, or things intended to be thought about, stands stiff and immutable like Plato's Realm of Ideas" (P, I, 462).

Here it is germane to remark that side by side with the phenomenological sort of reasoning behind James's epistemological revolution is another sort of reasoning – which may be called "metaphysical." Despite James's disclaimer that, bent on establishing psychology as a science, he is not doing metaphysics, throughout the *Principles* metaphysics keeps bursting out. Basically James's metaphysics is a flux or process philosophy. At the same time James acknowledged, above the flux, an order of permanent entities which the mind, by its intentions, carves out of the flux. Although for James the thinker is the passing thought (P, I, 342), what the thinker thinks is arrested by his intention and so rendered as a meaning absolutely immutable. Thus James's metaphysics of flux embraces also an eternal realm of conceptions. The Platonic (or rationalist) theme may seem alien to James's psychology; nonetheless it is a resident in his metaphysics of flux. No doubt, it has spread from James's philosophy and become full-grown in the realm of essence of George Santayana, James's most famous pupil. On his part James probably derived this dualistic metaphysics of experience in flux and of conceptions in eternity from Shadworth Hodgson, whom he cited in the chapter on conception as well as in other places throughout the *Principles*. For like Hodgson, he stressed that a conception is eternal, that it is what it is and is capable of becoming nothing else, in order to undercut the Hegelian dialectic of developing concepts forming a continuum. On James's theory no conception can develop or change into another; experience is the continuum and every conception is discrete; the mind in pursuit of its interests isolates in fixity parts of the flux for use in managing other parts of the flux and may, in the process, change from one set of fixed conceptions to another.[1] As James amplified:

> Every one of our conceptions is of something which our attention originally tore out of the continuum of felt experience, and provisionally isolated so as to make of it an individual topic of discourse...
> Conceptions form the one class of entities that cannot under any circumstances change. They can cease to be, altogether; or they can stay, as what they severally are; but there is for them no middle way. They form an essentially discontinuous system, and translate the process of our perceptual experience, which is naturally a flux, into a set of stagnant and petrified terms. The very conception of flux itself is an absolutely changeless meaning in the mind; it signifies just that one thing, flux, immovably (P, I, 465, 467–468).

The function of conception, moreover, is indifferent to the sort of content within the flux of experience upon which it seizes. As James said:

> Any fact, be it thing, event, or quality, may be conceived sufficiently for purposes of identification, if only it be singled out and marked so as to separate it from other things. Simply calling it 'this' or 'that' will suffice (P, I, 462).
> Our meanings are of singulars, particulars, indefinites, and universals, mixed together in every way. A singular individual is as much *conceived* when he is isolated and identified away from the rest of the world in my mind, as is the most rarefied and universally applicable quality he may possess – *being*, for example, when treated in the same way (P, I, 479).

A. The Realist-Nominalist Controversy Resolved

Most of Chapter XII on conception is devoted to James's treatment of the controversy between the nominalists and the realists. What James considered their mistakes to be and how he proposed to resolve their dispute throws additional light

---

[1] One scholar has detected here and in the final chapter of the *Principles* an anticipation of C. I. Lewis's pragmatic *a priori*. See Lillian Pancheri, "James, Lewis, and the Pragmatic A Priori," *Transactions of the Charles S. Peirce Society*, VII (1971), 135–149.

on his theory of conception. At the risk of digressing, then, we shall now consider James's treatment of this ancient controversy in the *Principles*.

The nominalists, James charged, wrongly assume that" we really never frame any conception of the partial elements of an experience, but are compelled, whenever we think it, to think it in its totality, just as it came" (P, I, 468). This assumption is wrong because it fails to distinguish the object of thought from the topic of thought. Consequently, it "amounts to saying that an idea must *be* a duplicate edition of what it knows – in other words, that it can only know itself – or, more shortly still, that knowledge in any strict sense of the word, as a self-transcendent function, is impossible" (P, I, 471). Thus however meshed the states in the continuum of experience may be, the mind may select and fix upon a part of the flux, and in doing so, it conceptualizes.

Against the nominalists, therefore, James upheld conceptualism. He declared: "Conceptualism says that the mind can conceive any quality or relation it pleases, and mean nothing but it in isolation from everything else in the world" (P, I, 470). To make a case for conceptualism James amplified his theory of conception.

Now it should be clear that for James the mind conceives when it attends to some part of the flowing continuum of experience and intends by means of the abstracted part some other parts of the continuum. Its conception is never required to be identical with its intended object, nor even to resemble this object. James said:

All that a state of mind need do, in order to take cognizance of a reality, intend it, or be 'about' it, is to lead to a remoter state of mind which either acts upon the reality or resembles it. The only class of thoughts which can with any show of plausibility be said to resemble their objects are sensations. The stuff of which all our other thoughts are composed is symbolic, and thought attests its pertinency to a topic by simply *terminating*, sooner or later, in a sensation which resembles the latter (P, I, 471).

Waiving for the present whether and how a sensation may resemble its object, we note now James's emphasis on the symbolic character of thought. He described this character as "one

of those evanescent and 'transitive' facts of mind which intro-
spection cannot turn round upon, and isolate and hold up for
examination, as an entomologist passes round an insect on a pin"
(P, I, 472). The phrases James employed to designate the symbolic character of thought are "the 'fringe' of the subjective
state" and "the feeling of tendency." According to James's
theory, then, a thought is situated in a stream of experience;
its nucleus is an image; but, instead of being sharply walled,
the image has a fringe. In regard to conception, the nucleus of
thought, the image, is less important than its fringe, for according to James, the fringe accounts for the fact that thought
is symbolic – i.e., cognitive. The fringe enables the thought,
composed of nuclear image plus fringe, to transcend itself.

James's theory of the "fringe" bears directly upon his
doctrine of universals. Since every thought selects a part from
a whole, according to James, all thought is abstract. A universal is a general thought, or conception; it is but one kind of
abstraction. As James wrote: "An individual conception is of
something restricted, in its application, to a single case. A
universal or general conception is of an entire class, or of something belonging to an entire class of things" (P, I, 473). It is
the fringe, or vague consciousness, surrounding an image which
enables thought, no matter how detailed as image it may be,
to stand for or symbolize a class of things, events, or qualities.

The realists, James charged, erroneously assume that for an
idea to know a universal it must be a universal. This assumption
is wrong because it confuses an idea with the object it knows,
a confusion avoidable so long as one consciously adheres to
epistemological dualism. A thought is always a particular
image plus fringe, no matter what its object may be. The
mistake of realism is rectified when the distinction James
made between the object of thought and the topic of thought
is adopted. The topic is a part of the object, a part selected by
the mind as that which it means or intends. As James said:
"The continuity and permanency of the topic is of the essence
of our intellection" (P, I, 481). Thus objects of thought may
always be concrete singulars, while some topics of thought are
universals.

Hence James approached the controversy over universals

from two sides. On the objective side, the topic accounts for the way the mind intends the same throughout the flux of experience. On the subjective side, the fringe accounts for the way a thought may transcend its particular image to denote a class of things. Thus the mind, governed by its topic, employs a thought, with an image at its nucleus and surrounded by a vague fringe, to stand for a class of other things, events, or qualities. Each member in the class is, of course, encrusted with the particular details of its place in the continuous flux of experience. Yet each may be singled out from the flux and classed together with others so far as each conforms to the topic of thought which isolates and classifies it.

Between realism and nominalism James took the route of conceptualism. But it is a unique brand of conceptualism. Specifically, James was careful to repudiate conceptualism in its nineteenth century form. He remarked that conceptualists are committed to a transcendental psychology which explains the knowledge of universals by invoking "an Ego, whose function is treated as quasi-miraculous and nothing if not awe-inspiring, and which it is a sort of blasphemy to approach with the intent to explain and make common, or reduce to lower terms" (P, I, 474). By contrast James, as scientific psychologist, stressed the physical basis of thought, pointing to neural and cerebral processes.

On this physical basis thought rests, but then it operates almost as the conceptualists minimally demand. In a passage which owes much to Shadworth Hodgson, James wrote:

The distinction between having and operating is as natural in the mental as in the material world. As our hands may hold a bit of wood and a knife, and yet do naught with either; so our mind may simply be aware of a thing's existence, and yet neither attend to it nor discriminate it, neither locate nor count nor compare nor like nor dislike nor deduce it, nor recognize it articulately as having been met with before. At the same time we know that, instead of staring at it in this entranced and senseless way, we may rally our activity in a moment, and locate, class, compare, count, and judge it. There is nothing involved in all this which we did not postulate at the very outset of our introspective work: realities, namely, *extra mentem*, thoughts, and possible relations of cognition between the two. The result of the thoughts' operating on the data given to sense is to transform the order in which experience *comes* into an entirely different order, that of the *conceived* world. ... The conceptual scheme is a sort of sieve in which we try to gather up the world's contents. Most facts and relations fall through its meshes, being either too subtle or insignificant to be fixed in any conception. But whenever a physical reality is caught and identified as the same with something already conceived, it remains on the sieve, and all the predicates and relations of the conception with which it is identified become its predicates and relations too; it is subjected to the sieve's network, in other words. Thus comes to pass what Mr. Hodgson calls the translation of the perceptual into the conceptual order of the world. (P, I, 481–482).

The translation, moreover, is not the product of a disinterested, disembodied mind. James declared in italics: *"This whole function of conceiving, of fixing, and holding fast to meanings, has no significance apart from the fact that the conceiver is a creature with partial purposes and private ends"* (P, I, 482).

B. Reasoning

James's theory of conception, while it provides for the creativity of mind featured in conceptualism, is rooted in a physical organism whose consciousness is functional to its survival and advance in nature. This theory of conception is further supported in Chapter XXII of the *Principles*, where James presented his view on reasoning, and, to some degree by implication, on logic.

James contended that "... all Reasoning depends on the ability of the mind to break up the totality of the phenomenon reasoned about, into parts, and to pick out from among these the particular one which, in our given emergency, may lead to the proper conclusion" (P, I, 287). He added: "Reasoning is but another form of the selective activity of the mind" (P, I, 287).

Now in Chapter XXII James distinguished two kinds of thought: Empirical Thought and Reasoned Thought. Brute animals have empirical thought; such thinking unfolds simply as the association of ideas. By contrast, man reasons as well, reasoned thought being most prominent in men of genius. Reasoned thought abstracts, classifies, and logically infers. James amplified:

Every phenomenon or so-called 'fact' has an infinity of aspects or properties ... amongst which the fool, or man with little sagacity, will inevitably go astray .... every possible case of reasoning involves the extraction of a particular partial aspect of the phenomena thought about, and ... whilst Empirical Thought simply associates phenomena in their entirety, Reasoned Thought couples them by the conscious use of this extract (P, II, 341).

Reasoning, then, operates by means of an extract which it selects. James's term for this extract, one borrowed from traditional philosophy, is "essence." However, it is necessary to remark that for James the essences of things are not absolute. On the objective side, the phenomena themselves display an infinity of qualities and properties, suggesting that no single one or set can constitute its absolute, objective essence. On the subjective side, the mind is dominated by its interests: "first, our practical or instinctive interests; and second, our aesthetic interests" (P, II, 344). These interests predispose the mind to attend to certain properties and to rely upon these properties in its reasoning. In a sentence which foreshadows his later pragmatism, James said: "My thinking is first and last and always for the sake of my doing, and I can only do one thing at a time" (P, II, 333). Now this sentence may be an overstatement, since in the previously quoted passage he did concede a place, though secondary, for aesthetic interests.

Hence for James the reasoning mind mutilates the fullness of phenomena to extract essences upon which it further reasons to satisfy its practical and aesthetic interests. As he said, "... the only meaning of essence is teleological, and ... classification and conception are purely teleological weapons of the mind" (P, II, 335). An essence, then, is relational rather than absolute; it is the way a property, itself immersed in a concrete totality within the flowing continuum of experience, is isolated by a consciousness dominated by non-cognitive interests.

To raise the question whether there is a check on the subjectivity of the reasoning mind is perhaps to miss the contextualist thesis which pervades James's discussion and to revert to the empirical emphasis with its quest for epistemological foundations. Nevertheless, guided – or misguided – by this question, we shall proceed to examine James's treatment of sensation, perception, belief, and truth in the *Principles*. Thus we will reach a balanced and comprehensive grasp of his epistemology.

VI. Sensation

There are many passages in the *Principles* in which the empirical emphasis is conspicuous, and wherever it is, sensations are asserted to be the bedrock of knowledge. Thus James wrote:

Conceptual systems which neither began nor left off in sensations would be like bridges without piers. Systems about fact must plunge themselves into sensation as bridges plunge their piers into the rock. Sensations are the stable rock, the *terminus ad quo* and the *terminus ad quem* of thought (P, II, 7).

Nevertheless, it would be wrong to conclude that James adhered strictly to the empiricist tenet that sensations are the bedrock of knowledge. After all, the *Principles* contains no chapter on the senses, although he supplied such chapters, mainly for commercial reasons, for his textbook abridgment, *Psychology, Briefer Course* (1892). In the *Principles* he explicitly justified the omission on the grounds that the senses find their proper place and are sufficiently well-treated in all the physiological books (P, II, 3). Furthermore, probably no empiricist epistemologist would elaborate, as James did, a theory of conception before one of sensation. Why did James do so? On the first page of Volume II of the *Principles*, also the first page of his chapter on sensation, James wrote: "After inner perception, outer perception!" Now James's claim that Volume I treats inner perception and Volume II outer perception, like his explicit justification for omitting chapters on the senses, is superficial, particularly since the second chapter of Volume II is devoted to imagination. Far deeper reasons were influencing James's program.

Essentially James was abandoning the theory of consciousness of traditional empiricism, with its stress on the special senses, for a new theory of consciousness based on the brain and the central nervous system. Consistently, the first two chapters of the *Principles* are devoted to the brain and brain-activities. These chapters are prerequisite to all that follows, although they, no less than the omitted chapters on the senses, contain material that could have been found in books on physiology. In sum, James had found the path to a new psychology in which cognition is not constructed out of sensory elements, as traditional empiricism asserted. In the new psychology the empiricist emphasis is displaced by the contextualist thesis.

Now James replaced the atomic sensationalism of traditional empiricism with his own doctrine of the stream of consciousness, a doctrine which I have discussed elsewhere.[1] The implication of this doctrine for the theory of sensations is far-reaching. The repudiation of psychological atomism is at one with James's assertion: "No one ever had a simple sensation by itself" (P, I, 224). Of course in a later passage James did suggest that the first sensation of a new-born baby might qualify as simple. The new-born baby, James surmised, receives strong messages from the sense-organs, and so experiences "an absolutely pure sensation" (P, II, 8). But the next experience cannot be a pure sensation, since his brain has been affected by the first experience in such a way that the sensation is no longer pure. Furthermore, the original sensation is no discrete sensation, nor even a mere aggregate of discrete sensations. It is far richer than traditional empiricism with its doctrine of atomic sensationalism held. As James put the matter: "The baby, assailed by eyes, ears, nose, skin, and entrails at once, feels it all as one great blooming, buzzing, confusion . . . ." (P, I, 488).

Now traditional empiricism affirms that sensations link consciousness directly with reality. The linkage, furthermore, is both causal and cognitive. Objects cause sensations, and by means of sensations consciousness knows objects. In his treatment of truth above, James considered the resemblance of an idea with reality to be one criterion of truth, and he also seemed to suggest that sensations resemble reality – indeed, that

[1] See Andrew J. Reck, *Introduction to William James* (Bloomington: Indiana University Press, 1967), pp. 28–29.

resemblance is primarily a relation between sensory ideas and their objects. But in fact James's position on the linkage between sensations and reality in the *Principles* is exceedingly hedged.

James claimed that all schools of thought "must allow that the *elementary qualities* of cold, heat, pleasure, pain, red, blue, sound, silence, etc., are original, innate, or *a priori* properties of our subjective nature, even though they should require the touch of experience to waken them into actual consciousness and should slumber, to all eternity, without it" (P, II, 618). He justified this claim by reflection.

... on either of the two hypotheses we may make concerning the relation of feelings to the realities at whose touch they become alive. For in the first place, if a feeling do *not* mirror the reality which wakens it and to which we say it corresponds, if it mirror no reality whatever outside of the mind, it of course is a purely mental product. By its very definition it can be nothing else. But in the second place, even if it *do* mirror the reality exactly, still it *is* not that reality itself, it is a duplication of it, the result of a mental reaction. And that the mind should have the power of reacting in just that duplicate way can only be stated as a *harmony* between its nature and the nature of the truth outside of it, a harmony whereby it follows that the qualities of both parties match (P, II. 618).

Later, when treating the so-called elementary categories, among which sensation is listed first, James denied that they are mere impressions of objects upon consciousness. Of the original elements of consciousness, such as sensation, time, and space, James admitted as plausible the hypothesis that, instead of being the sensible presence of objects, they are "pure *idiosyncrasies*, spontaneous variations, fitted by good luck (those of them which have survived) to take cognizance of objects (that is, to steer us in our active dealings with them), without being in any intelligible sense immediate derivatives from them" (P, II, 631). He amplified:

All these elements are subjective duplicates of outer objects. They *are* not the outer objects. The secondary qualities among them are not supposed by any educated person even to resemble the objects. Their *nature* depends more on the reacting brain than on the stimuli which touch it off (P, II, 631).

Thus James's treatment of sensations exhibits both his empiricist emphasis and his contextualist thesis. When the empiricist emphasis is prominent, sensations are asserted to be the bedrock of knowledge. It is even suggested that sensations resemble their objects, in conformity to the realistic epistemological dualism which James assumed. Upon examination, however, it proves untenable to hold that the contents of sensations resemble their objects, for these contents are subjective. Sensations are said to be *duplicates* – rather than to *resemble* – their objects, and the duplicates are qualified essentially as subjective. Further, in the treatment of sensation, the contextualist thesis prevailed over the empiricist emphasis when James contended that sensation is never absolute or pure, except in the first experience of the new-born baby.

VII. Perception

James's contextualism in the *Principles* is manifest in the way he distinguished sensation from perception. Remarking that in ordinary language these words are not sharply discriminated, James noted:

Both of them name processes in which we cognize an objective world; both (under normal conditions) need the stimulation of incoming nerves ere they can occur; Perception always involves Sensation as a portion of itself; and Sensation in turn never takes place in adult life without Perception also being there. They are therefore names for different cognitive *functions*, not for different sorts of mental *fact*. The nearer the object cognized comes to being a simple quality like 'hot,' 'cold,' 'red,' 'noise,' 'pain,' apprehended irrelatively to other things, the more the state of mind approaches pure sensation. The fuller of relations the object is, on the contrary; the more it is something classed, located, measured, compared, assigned to a function, etc., etc.; the more unreservedly do we call the state of mind a perception, and the relatively smaller is the part in it which sensation plays.

Sensation, then, so long as we take the analytic point of view, differs from Perception only in the extreme simplicity of its object or content. Its function is that of mere *acquaintance* with a fact. Perception's function, on the other hand, is knowledge *about* a fact; and this knowledge admits of numberless degrees of complication (P, II, 1–2).

James's reference to two kinds of knowledge is explicit in this passage. Sensation is knowledge of acquaintance, and perception, knowledge-about. The object of sensation is a simple quality, whereas the object of perception is full of relations. However, James maintained that sensation and perception signify different cognitive functions. Not separate mental facts, sensation blurs into perception; so that the same fact may be sensed or perceived, depending upon the degree to which it is apprehended in relation to other things.

James, of course, found similarity as well as difference between sensation and perception. Characteristically he appealed to physiology to explain the similarity and the difference. He said:

... in both sensation and perception we perceive the fact as an *immediately* present outward reality, and this makes them differ from 'thought' and 'conception,' whose objects do not appear present in this immediate physical way. *From the physiological point of view both sensations and perceptions differ from 'thoughts'* (in the narrower sense of the word) *in the fact that nerve-currents coming in from the periphery are involved in their production. In perception these nerve-currents arouse voluminous associative or reproductive processes in the cortex; but when sensation occurs alone, or with a minimum of perception, the accompanying reproductive processes are at a minimum too* (P, II, 2–3).

Physiology, then, explains how sensation in adult experience is incorporated directly into perception. The consequence for epistemology is that no absolute distinction can be made between perception and sensation. As James said,

A pure sensation ... (is) an abstraction never realized in adult life. Any quality of a thing which affects our sense-organs does also more than that: it arouses processes in the hemispheres (of the brain) which are due to the organization of that organ by past experiences, and the results of which in consciousness are commonly described as ideas which the sensation suggests. The first of these ideas is that of the *thing* to which the sensible quality belongs. *The consciousness of particular material things present to sense* is nowadays called *perception*. The consciousness of such things may be more or less complete; it may be of the mere name of the thing and its other essential attributes, or it may be of the thing's various remoter relations. It is impossible to draw any sharp line of distinction between the barer and the richer consciousness, because the moment we get beyond the first crude sensation all our consciousness is a matter of suggestion, and the various suggestions shade gradually into each other, being one and all products of the same psychological machinery of association. In the directer consciousness fewer, in the remoter more, associative processes are brought into play.

Perception thus differs from sensation by consciousness of farther facts associated with the object of the sensation... (P, II, 76–77).

After showing how sensation shades into perception, James turned next to an investigation of perception as it functions in regard to things, space, time, and reality. Just as no sharp epistemological distinction can be drawn between sensation and perception, none can be drawn between perception and belief. For James, perception of reality is belief.

VIII. Belief

In 1889 in the July issue of *Mind* James published an article, entitled "The Psychology of Belief." This article is reprinted, with revisions and additions, as Chapter XXI of the *Principles*. The title of Chapter XXI is "Perception of Reality."

James's theory of belief owes much to the protophenomenologist Franz Brentano, whose *Psychologie* he cited and quoted (P, II, 286). Sensation, perception, conception point to or intend objects. Every cognitive state of consciousness refers to objects, and so transcends itself. Reference to objects is one of the five distinctive marks of consciousness according to James. Yet, following Brentano, James distinguished conception from belief. In the case of conception, the object is merely apprehended by the mind. In the case of belief, it is also "held to have reality. Belief is thus the mental state or function of cognizing reality" (P, II, 286). Belief, then, and not conception, affords a cognitive route to reality; but the route is hardly a straight and narrow path. For James considered belief to be the natural condition of the human mind. Thus any object, if and so long as it is uncontradicted, is believed and so regarded to be real.

James depicted seven sub-universes of reality. Every object of thought belongs to one or other of these universes. These universes of reality are:

(1) The world of sense, or of physical 'things' as we instinctively apprehend them...
(2) The world of science, or of physical things as the learned conceive them...
(3) The world of ideal relations, or abstract truths believed or believable by all, and expressed in logical, mathematical, metaphysical, ethical, or aesthetic propositions.
(4) The world of 'idols of the tribe,' illusions or prejudices common to the race...
(5) The various supernatural worlds...
(6) The various worlds of individual opinion, as numerous as men are.
(7) The worlds of sheer madness and vagary, also indefinitely numerous ... (P, II, 292–293).

Any object of thought may be real if it is also an object of belief. Its reality, however, is contextual in the sense that it is dependent upon the mental act of belief and also its logical locus in one of the seven universes. As James remarked, "Each world *whilst it is attended to* is real after its own fashion; only the reality lapses with the attention" (P, II, 293).

The question arises: What is real? James's answer pointed to the individual's choice according to his interests as the practical criterion of reality. He wrote:

The mere fact of appearing as an object at all is not enough to constitute reality. That may be metaphysical reality, reality for God; but what we need is practical reality, reality for ourselves; and, to have that, an object must not only appear, but it must appear both *interesting* and *important*. The worlds whose objects are neither interesting nor important we treat simply negatively, we brand them as *un*real.

In the relative sense, then, the sense in which we contrast reality with simple *un*reality, and in which one thing is said to have *more* reality than another, and to be more believed, *reality means simply relation to our emotional and active life.* This is the only sense which the word ever has in the mouths of practical men. *In this sense, whatever excites and stimulates our interest is real* ... (P, II, 295).

Of course James remained under the influence of the empiricist emphasis when he acknowledged "the paramount reality of sensations" (P, II, 299–306). His account of sensations in regard to belief in reality owes much to Locke and Hume, and at the same time presages his later pragmatism. He wrote:

Sensible objects are thus either our realities or the tests of our realities. Conceived objects must show sensible effects or else be disbelieved...

Sensible vividness or pungency is then the vital factor in reality when once the conflict between objects, and the connecting of them together in the mind, has begun (P, II, 301).

Moreover, even as James stressed "the prerogative position of sensations in regard to our belief," he interjected the contextualist thesis, remarking that "among the sensations themselves all are not deemed equally real. The more practically important ones, the more permanent ones, and the more aesthetically apprehensible ones are selected from the mass, to be believed in most of all; the others are degraded to the position of mere signs and suggestions of these" (P, II, 305). And in support of his contextualistic view of the sensations he cited and quoted a major – perhaps the major – figure of traditional empiricism: "Among all sensations, the *most* belief-compelling are those productive of pleasure or of pain. Locke expressly makes the *pleasure*-or-*pain*-giving quality to be the ultimate human criterion of anything's reality" (P, II, 306).

James's discussion of belief opens with a protophenomenological analysis; it continues in the direction of empiricism; and it ends on a voluntaristic note suggesting a metaphysics presupposed. While for James knowledge is dualistic, relating subject and object, the interests are central in establishing the relation and in imbuing the object with reality. Although every thought has an object, belief consists in the emotional reaction of the entire man toward this object, whatever it may be. Thus belief is one with will. As James emphasized: *"Will and Belief, in short, meaning a certain relation between objects and the Self, are two names for one and the same PSYCHOLOGICAL phenomenon"* (P, II, 321).

IX. Necessary Truths

In the final chapter of the *Principles of Psychology* James presented a theory of necessary truth. Only recently have scholars attended to this part of James's epistemology.[1] It

---

[1] See Lillian Pancheri, *op. cit.*, and also the very suggestive discussion by Morton White, *Science and Sentiment in America* (New York: Oxford University Press, 1972), pp. 172–180.

represents a rationalist thread in James's theory of knowledge, a rationalist thread which runs through his treatment of conceptions, from his view that they are immutable like Platonic entities to the thesis that certain of their relations are *a priori*. In the latter regard, he contended that there are *a priori* (or rational) propositions, and furthermore that some of these propositions are true.

Although the very title of the final chapter – "Necessary Truths and the Effects of Experience" – suggests that there is a connection between these truths and experience, in accord with the requirements of empiricism, James adamantly rejected the empiricism – or as he called it, "the experience-philosophy" – prevalent in the nineteenth century, championed by Stuart Mill in the name of individual experience and by Herbert Spencer in the name of radical experience. James was careful to define what he meant by the word "experience." He wrote in italics: *"Experience means experience of something foreign supposed to impress us ...."* (P, II, 619). Necessary truths, James maintained, are not derived from experience in this sense. In presenting his theory James again appealed to the authority of John Locke. He said, "... in truth I have done nothing more ... than to make a little more explicit the teachings of Locke's fourth book [in the *Essay concerning Human Understanding*]" (P, II, 662).

James offered a naturalistic account of the origin of the *a priori*. He placed the brain, a physical organ, in the center of the cognitional process. On the one side are external objects impressing the senses – experience in the strict sense. On the other side are causes operating within the physical organism and, in particular, within the brain. Sensory experience, so to speak, comes in the front door, whereas necessary truths are "born in the house" (P, II, 627). Thus James gave a psychogentic explanation of the *a priori* which rejected Spencer's interpretation of evolution in favor of Darwin's.

According to Spencer, the mind passively adapts to its environment, and knowledge consists in the conformity of inner relations to outer relations. Necessary truths are the result of racial memory. Our remote ancestors, having always experienced certain fixed connections between phenomena, formulated truths which have been transmitted to us within our memories and so are *a priori* for each individual mind. Against Spencer James argued that the *a priori* is not impressed upon the mind from outside but is brain-born.

While James conceded that in the case of our cognition of space and time the inner relations are stamped on our minds from the outside (P, II, 632), he argued that in regard to the other mental categories and their interrelations, their origin is due to the mind and not to experience. Consider the difference between even such empirical qualities as "black" and "white." James observed:

> To learn whether black and white differ, I need not consult the world of experience at all; the mere ideas suffice. *What I mean* by black differs from what I mean by white, whether such colors exist *extra mentem meam* or not. If they ever do so exist, they *will* differ. White things may blacken, but the black of them will differ from the white of them, so long as I mean anything definite by these three words (P, II, 643–644).

Hence James stressed the activity of the mind as the source of the *a priori*. Nevertheless, he was careful to repudiate the Kantian doctrine that the mind legislates over experience and nature. In a revealing footnote he refrained from engaging in "the old debate as to whether the *a priori* truths are 'analytic' or 'synthetic'" with the remark "that the distinction is one of Kant's most unhappy legacies, for the reason that it is impossible to make it sharp" (P, II, 661n). James's position is a noteworthy anticipation of the recent views of W.V. Quine and Morton White. Upon James's analysis, every so-called analytic judgment violates the Kantian criterion for analyticity, since it is ampliative in the sense that its predicate is "a somewhat new way of conceiving as well as of naming the subject" (P, II, 661n). Hence, "the question 'at what point does the new state of mind cease to be implicit in the old?' is too vague to be answered" (P, II, 662n). For James, therefore, all propositions are synthetic. As he said,

> The only sharp way of defining synthetic propositions would be to say that they express a relation between *two data* at least. But it is hard to find any proposition which cannot be construed as doing this. Even verbal propositions do it (P, II, 662n).

It is James's conception of the role of the *a priori* in regard to experience which renders for him the debate as to whether it is synthetic or analytic wholly meaningless. As James said,

> All philosophic interest vanishes from the question, the moment one ceases to ascribe to *any a priori* truths (whether analytic or synthetic) that 'legislative character for all possible experience' which Kant believed in. We ourselves have denied such legislative character, and contended that it was for experience itself to prove whether its data can or cannot be assimilated to those ideal terms between which *a priori* relations obtain. The analytic-synthetic debate is thus for us devoid of all significance (P, II, 662n).

Now James acknowledged a large class of *a priori* truths (rational propositions) in contradistinction to empirical propositions. The *a priori* propositions arise not from experience, but from the "native structure" of the human mind, "in this sense, that certain of its objects, if considered together in certain ways, give definite results; and that no other ways of considering, and no other results, are possible if the same objects be taken" (P, II, 276). These results are simply relations between conceptions which judgments of subsumption and of comparison express.

Unsurprisingly, logic and mathematics consist of *a priori* propositions which express such relations. Classifications, too, derive from judgments of comparison and consequently generate propositions which are *a priori*. Dependent on classification and incorporating logic and mathematics, natural science is shot through with *a priori* propositions. Here conspicuously displayed is what Morton White calls "rationalism" in James's epistemology in the *Principles*. Nor can the rational order which natural science represents be reduced to the empirical order of things and events in space and time. This sort of reduction is what empiricists and positivists in quest for the unity of science have usually demanded. But for James, at least in the last chapter of the *Principles*, natural science advances by means of the reverse procedure – namely, by translating the empirical order into the rational order. And the rational order springs not from experience but from the structure of the mind. Thus James amplified:

Any classification of things into kinds (especially if the kinds form series, or if they successively involve each other) is a more rational way of conceiving the things than is that mere juxtaposition or separation of them as individuals in the time and space which is the order of their crude perception. Any assimilation of terms between which such classificatory relations, with their remote and mediate transactions, obtain, is a way of bringing the things into a more rational scheme.

Solids in motion are such terms; and the mechanical philosophy is only a way of conceiving nature so as to arrange its items along some of the more natural lines of cleavage of our mental structure (P, II, 676–677).

Metaphysical, moral, and aesthetic propositions are also, for James, *a priori* propositions, originating in the structure of the human mind. The ideal relations expressed by such metaphysical axioms as "the Principle of things is one" or "Nature acts by the shortest ways" generate what James called "*postulates of rationality,* not propositions of fact. If nature *did* obey them, she *would* be *pro tanto* more intelligible; and we seek meanwhile so to conceive her phenomena as to show that she does obey them" (P, II, 670). Moral and aesthetic relations have a similar status. James wrote:

Philosophy is still seeking to conceive things so that these relations also may seem to obtain between them.

As long as things have not successfully been so conceived, the moral and aesthetic relations obtain only between *entia rationis*, terms in the mind; and the moral and aesthetic principles remain, but postulates, not propositions, with regard to the real outside (P, II, 677).

For James, therefore, the *a priori*, embracing necessary truths in logic and mathematics, empirically applicable theories in natural science, and postulates in metaphysics, morals, and aesthetics, originates in the structure of the human mind. Although the *a priori* neither comes from experience whether individual or racial nor merely traces the sequence of outer relations or the associations of empirical data, it nevertheless has a natural basis. For the mind is embodied, and the *a priori* is "brain-born" (P, II, 639).

James's description of the mechanism by which the brain develops into an organ with the sort of mental structure requisite to the kinds of *a priori* propositions there are leans heavily upon the Darwinian theory of evolution by accidental variations and natural selection. Neither a transcendental ego legislating for nature and experience, nor a passive mirror of its environment, the mind is dynamically related to the brain. A conception of mental structure, to be scientifically valid, must refer to the structure of the brain, which indeed is the ultimate foundation of the *a priori*. James wrote:

What happens in the brain after experience has done its utmost is what happens in every material mass which has been fashioned by an outward force, – in every pudding or mortar, for example, which I may make with my hands. The fashioning from without brings the elements into collocations which set new internal forces free to exert their effects in turn. And the random irradiations and resettlements of our ideas, which *supervene upon experience*, and constitute our free mental play, are due entirely to these secondary internal processes, which vary enormously from brain to brain, even though the brains be exposed to exactly the same 'outer relations.' The higher thought processes owe their being to causes which correspond far more to the sourings and fermentations of dough, the setting of mortar, or the subsidence of sediments in mixtures, than to the manipulations by which these physical aggregates came to be compounded (P, II, 638).

X. *Conclusions*

The present study of the epistemology in James's *Principles of Psychology* has traversed a wide compass of subjects. It is proper to close by focussing on some main results of the investigation.

1) James was an agent of the twentieth century revolution in epistemology. Instead of seeking to justify knowledge, he assumed that there is knowledge and concentrated on the task of criticizing and analyzing knowledge. But he performed these critical and analytical tasks of a revolutionized epistemology within the framework of psychology as a natural science.

2) James also assumed in the *Principles* an epistemological dualism. Thus he accepted the distinction between an idea and its object and he held knowledge to consist in the correspondence of an idea and its object. He considered epistemological dualism to be a useful instrument in clearing away the confusions generated by "the psychologist's fallacy." On one hand, he held that knowledge leads directly to situations in

which the idea corresponds to its object. On the other, he invoked the mind of the psychologist to provide the standpoint from which to compare the idea with is object.

3) The requirement that knowledge be analyzed into ideas which ultimately lead to objects given in experience is the empiricist emphasis discernible in James's epistemology. It is operative, to some extent, in James's pioneering distinction between knowledge of acquaintance and knowledge-about. When drawing this distinction James suggested that knowledge-about – i.e., conceptual knowledge – has its basis in knowledge of acquaintance – i.e., direct or immediate experience. However, James did not intend to draw an absolute distinction, as his text makes plain. What is knowledge of acquaintance and what is knowledge-about are contextually determined. Thus the empiricist emphasis yields to the contextualist thesis. Whereas the empiricist emphasis demands that knowledge have absolute foundations in direct or immediate experience, the contextualist thesis abandons altogether the quest for absolute foundations for knowledge, holding instead that what is epistemologically basic varies from situation to situation.

4) Two sorts of reasoning underlie the emerging contextualism in the epistemology of James's *Principles:* 1) phenomenological, and 2) metaphysical. Phenomenological reasoning is apparent whenever, in the analysis of knowledge, James appealed to the activities or the structure of the mind. It is paramount in his theories of conception, of belief, and of necessary truths. Metaphysical reasoning crops up again and again throughout the *Principles*, despite James's intermittent efforts to exclude metaphysics. Such reasoning is manifest in James's claims that experience (or reality) is a plenum in flux, that belief in reality is ultimately dependent upon the will (with reality having different contextual meanings according to the interests which dominate the will), and that the crux of mind is the brain, an organ of an organism evolving in nature according to the Darwinian principles of accidental variations and natural selection. Although both the phenomenology and the metaphysics in James's *Principles* are beyond the compass of the present essay, it is clear now that the investigation of

these topics should proceed from the general understanding that James was first and foremost a scientific psychologist who had no use for transcendental psychology and its vagaries.

5) The dominant trait of James's epistemology in the *Principles* is the contextualist thesis, and not the empiricist emphasis. James's theory of conception as teleological and his resolution of the nominalist-realist controversy anticipate his later pragmatism without its nods to positivism and nominalism. By means of careful analytic and protophenomenological distinctions, such as "fringe," "object of thought," and "topic of thought," James sought to show how a content of consciousness could become for the mind a sense datum or a conception. Conception and empirical datum, then, are contextually distinguished according to the activities of the mind. Furthermore, James drew no sharp distinction between sensation and perception, denying indeed that pure sensation can exist in adult experience, and he even held that perception itself shades off into belief.

6) However, once there are concepts, according to James, they constitute a kind of realm of meanings which, like Platonic entities, are immutable. The relations between conceptions – at least, the relations of comparison and subsumption – are represented in propositions which are nothing less than necessary truths. Thus James's contextualism contains a rationalist theme side by side with its empiricist emphasis. The rationalist theme is crystallized in his theory of the *a priori*. According to this theory, there are rational propositions in logic, mathematics, natural science, metaphysics, morals, and aesthetics which come not from experience but from the structure of the human mind.

7) For James the mind is embodied – indeed resident in the brain. Although the centrality of the brain to James's epistemology in the *Principles* rules out immaterialistic and non-scientific interpretations of his thought, it is puzzling. As James himself confessed,

... thoughts accompany the brain's workings, and those thoughts are cognitive of realities. The whole relation is one which we can only write down empirically, confessing that no glimmer of explanation of it is yet in sight. That brains should give rise to a knowing consciousness at all, this is the one mystery which returns, no matter of what sort the consciousness and of what sort the knowledge may be (P, I, 687).

GEORGE BARTON AND THE ART OF TEACHING

LOUISE N. ROBERTS

Tulane University

The "art of teaching" is such a commonplace of academic
parlance that one rarely questions the significance of the
phrase. It is simply assumed that the word "art" refers to a
certain skill or *techne* which may, and hopefully shall, be
employed in the educational process. To pursue the meaning
further might lead to involvement in many of the theoretical
complexities of a philosophy of art, to say nothing of the
theory of teaching. It is probably safer to restrict the reference
to some sort of practice of teaching and leave the matter at
that. It is a temptation, however, to explore a few of the
questions which may escape from this box of Pandora. Some
of the most elusive of these concern the object or objects of
such an art. If the teacher is an artist in the sense of being a
maker, what does he make? Does the art of teaching have an
object not simply in the sense of being directed toward an end,
but also in the sense of achieving a skill-fully-made product?
If so, what is it? ... and how can it be employed as evidence
indicative of the skill of its producer? What a boon it would
be to administrators confronted by the practical problems of
evaluating academic performance if these questions could be
given straight-forward, unequivocal answers! Unfortunately,
such is not the present state of affairs.

Of course, it can be argued that the final product of the art
of teaching is the well-taught student and one might proceed
to test him accordingly in order to determine the skill of his
master. Are we to say, therefore, that the student is an object
of art? This suggests all sorts of relationships from the creation
of Galatea to the construction of Frankenstein, and undoubtedly analogous productions have been known to occur
within the teaching profession. Is the artist, therefore, to be

held responsible for his products? Are we to judge Socrates by Alcibiades or Aristotle by Alexander? Of course, every artist this side of the Almighty has his failures, but how are we to identify the successes? Who are the *well*-taught? Questions regarding the "art" of teaching have simply changed locus with consideration of the student as art object.

I would suggest that, accepting the "well-taught student", whoever that may be, as the end product of the art of teaching, there are still other objective factors within this production which are worthy of consideration as objects of the teaching art and which can offer evidence of the skill of the artist. Of particular interest among these "art objects" is what Beardsley, apologizing for his use of a "somewhat tainted contemporary term," has spoken of as the "educational scenario," i.e. the "advance plan or design for an educational experience or a sequence of educational experiences."[1] A plan of study can be looked upon as an object of the teaching art. Although not the end object of teaching, it is a product of technique and often an essential means to the ultimate achievement. Furthermore, it is less ephemeral than a given educational experience and is not entirely subject to the vagaries of particular students. Like a scenario or a musical score it can be experienced by a number of individuals in various contexts so that the value it possesses can become generally apparent. Professor George Barton's plan of readings for the Introduction to Philosophy is an example of such an object of art.

An academic course may take any one of a number of forms, many of which prompt analogies with performing arts such as music or drama. It has been suggested that education is itself "a mode of performance – that it is, indeed, at once the protean form and the apotheosis of performance. To pursue an education is to engage in the art of performing. We become educated just to the degree that we become accomplished performers of ourselves."[2] Perhaps the most familiar tradi-

[1] Monroe C. Beardsley, "Aesthetic Theory and Educational Theory," *Aesthetic Concepts and Education*, ed. Ralph A. Smith (Urbana, Illinois: University of Illinois Press, 1970), p. 5.
[2] Iredell Jenkins, "Performance", *Aesthetic Concepts and Education*, ed. Ralph A. Smith (Urbana, Illinois: University of Illinois Press, 1970. p, 212.

tional form of presentation is the solo performance in which the star not only dominates the stage but provides his own script, success often depending upon histrionic talent as well as the content of the course. More recently, however, there has been a tendency in some circles to reject the star system and to demand a more open, democratic situation so that the course more nearly resembles a series of happenings than a formal organic whole possessed of middle, beginning and end, to say nothing of plot. A possible mean between these extremes would be a course in which open class room discussion is based upon a shared structure of material. In such a course the "educational scenario" is fundamental. It provides a basic formal organization as well as a definite range of problems and a common vocabulary to be used by the "performers" who make up the class.[1] In the hands of a competent director it can make all of the difference between a series of impromptu classroom acts and a meaningful educational dialogue.

Of course the shared material along with the structure of a discussion course can be provided by any one of a number of recent popular textbooks, many of which are very well written. In such a case, a large part of the "art" involved in the teaching of the course is to be attributed to the author of the text. In the field of philosophy, however, there are also works by major thinkers which possess an intellectual depth and quality that defies contemporary paraphrase. There are classics which can provide the foundation for a course of study. Among these is Plato's *Republic*, in itself an ideal model of the educational experience.

The *Republic* has long been a popular text for the introduction to philosophy at Newcomb College. It offers a sort of conceptual Rorschach test in which one not only finds an exploration of perennial philosophical questions but may also discover insights regarding the particular issues with which one happens to be concerned at the time of reading. Like Philosophy herself, it is both ancient and forever young. It permits development within a framework of classical thought.

There are many ways of reading the *Republic* in an intro-

---

[1] *Ibid.*

ductory course. It can, for example, be part of a dialectic in which one text is used to "argue" against another in a chronological order. But, as Professor George Barton has shown in his development of the Introduction to Philosophy, it can also be used to function as a single structure extending through a semester. It can provide a broad pattern for discussion into which various additional readings are introduced in order to extend the arguments of Plato. Perhaps this method could be described as a series of variations upon motifs to be found within a classic work.

Let us consider the summary of a "scenario" developed by George Barton as a structure of assigned readings for an introductory course. At the opening of the *Republic* the class is introduced to the character of Socrates; among the themes to be found in his courteous exchange with Cephalus, his elderly host, is the evaluation of a total life. We are led to become better acquainted with Socrates, learn of his encounters with Athenian "justice", and share his own reflections at the end of life through reading Plato's *Apology* along with the *Crito*. We return to the *Republic* only to be confronted by Thrasymachus whose view of justice we then find exemplified in *The Prince* by Machiavelli. We learn, among other things, that the prince must seem to possess moral virtues but be prepared not to practice them and to change to the opposite when necessary. So it is that the way is prepared for a discussion of appearances and the Ring of Gyges. As the *Republic* proceeds in the pursuit of "justice", Socrates and Glaucon conjecture as to the genesis of the state and a simple economic foundation of society is described as providing for man's most basic animal needs. At this point we turn to *The Communist Manifesto* and in opposition to Plato's utopia of three classes united through a vision of the Good we find the vision of a classless society resting upon an ideal of economic justice. Dewey's *Moral Principles in Education* provides us with a foil for the carefully censored elementary education of Plato's future guardians, and Freud's Lecture XXXI, "Anatomy of Mental Personality", forces us to rethink Plato's tripartite division of the soul. Plato's "digression" concerning the role of women in his ideal state opens the way to class reports on contemporary views as to the place of women in society and in the structure of the family, a topic of particular concern in a college for women. As Plato develops his concept of the philosopher king and the true philosopher, we turn to *The Public Philosophy* and find Lippman describing Socrates as a man ruled within by his "second and civilized nature", the image of a man "who has become fit to rule." Through his figures of the divided line and the allegory of the cave, Plato's *Republic* offers us a theory of knowledge and of the relation upon which it is based. The ideal leader, the philosopher king, will be a man of vision, a man who possesses knowledge. We turn to the *Meno* and here we find similar theories of knowledge, but now they are set within the context of the problem of whether virtue can be taught. Who are they that possess the requisite knowledge to be our teachers? Who is to teach virtue to the sons of Pericles? In Plato's *Republic* we find that future leaders of the state would be given advanced training in mathematics and dialectic leading to a realization of the forms. They would move from a grasp of names to a knowledge of realities, as we learn from reading a selection from the *Seventh Epistle*. As we follow Plato's description of decline from perfection, we find models that seem more closely related to our empirical world of states and men. We read Tocqueville's description of our own democracy and consider his fears of a democratic form of tyranny. We then study an account of the last days of Hitler and weigh the values to be found in a life of despotism. Next, in opposition to Plato's highly debatable condemnation of the arts in the ideal state, we read one of his own artistic masterpieces, the *Symposium*. Here we find Plato's aesthetics of beauty which offers a challenge to any creative artist. Finally, as the *Republic* closes with the myth of Er and Plato reminds us of the responsibilities of our choice of life, we read Book V, Ch. V of *The Brothers Karamazov*, "The Grand Inquisitor". We are left to be haunted by Dostoevski's vision of the temptations and the dreadful responsibilities of leadership and freedom together with the values upon which they depend.

This brief outline does no more than indicate a pattern of reading and suggest a few of the relationships to be found within it. The possibilities of such a pattern of study are inestimable. Their realization depends not only upon the students, but also upon the socratic art of the teacher of such a course. Dr. George Barton is an experienced master of this art as well as the art of course planning. Through his technique, Plato's *Republic* is converted into a living contemporary dialogue enriched by a wealth of ideas drawn from the past and present, an educational experience in which knowledge comes but wisdom lingers.

DEWEY'S TRANSITION PIECE: THE *REFLEX ARC* PAPER

ALLEN K. SMITH

One of the most perplexing aspects of the study of recent American philosophy is the fact that pertinent information regarding the course of its development is sometimes as little known as that concerning thinkers historically as remote from us as the pre-Socratics. A case in point is the identification of the time and the place of John Dewey's metamorphosis from the Hegelianism in which he had been steeped into the propounder of his own distinctive brand of naturalism, which he later labeled 'instrumental pragmatism'. Dewey had not effected a break of any significance from the sway which the older philosophy exercised over him during his undergraduate studies at the University of Vermont, or while being influenced by the notable Hegelian G. S. Morris at the Johns Hopkins University, or even while on the faculties of the Universities of Michigan and Minnesota. This break occurred while he served as chairman of the Department of Philosophy, Psychology and Pedagogy at the University of Chicago, specifically with the work he published in the year 1896, "The Reflex Arc Concept in Psychology."[1]

Works composed before, such as his somewhat influential *Psychology*, for example, published in 1887 while Dewey was an associate professor at Michigan, deviate only slightly from an orthodox Hegelian orientation. Those works published after it break away. While Dewey's Reflex Arc paper ostensibly appears to be a straightforward critique of psychological investigations carried out during the latter part of the 19th century, it involves a good deal more than this. A close study will show that it was not any *specific* psychological theory that

[1] John Dewey, "The Reflex Arc Concept in Psychology," *Psychological Review*, III (July, 1896), 357–370.

Dewey was taking to task. Rather, it was deeply entrenched *philosophical* misconceptions inherent in the formulation employed by psychologists to order relevant data which were his concern. These misconceptions were simply manifestations of doctrines of classical philosophy in a disguised form applied to the solution of problems in methodology precipitated by contemporary scientific upheaval. With these considerations in mind, the aims of the present paper are twofold: (1) to present Dewey's criticism of the reflex arc concept, along with its deeper and more important philosophical implications; and (2) briefly to demonstrate that the philosophical tenets advanced by Dewey in the Reflex Arc paper represent a beginning for the comprehensive system of pragmatic philosophy which he formulated later.

Associationalism, in following the tradition of empirical philosophy by atomizing the mind and reducing it to elementary particles of sensation, created some unfortunate problems. By reducing the mind to discrete particles of sensation, associational psychology introduced the need of a purely *formal* associating-comparing activity, or source of ideas, available in order that the *material* sensations be related, combined and conceptualized into meaningful units. Unfortunately under the associationist schema the strictly formal ideas are superinduced *upon* the materials of sense *ab extra* in order externally to form them into meaningful and understandable units and are totally separate in nature from the material sensations.[2] Just as the elementary particles have to be brought together "from the outside," so do the discrete and incongruent parts of the mind: ideas on the one hand and sensations on the other. Thus, associational psychology created a dichotomy or bifurcation of a formal element and a material one. It vacillated between two alternative though equally untenable positions: (1) the belief that, through the use of an inventive enough schema, the two parts could be fused into a mind that is a singular, homogeneous whole; or (2) the two parts could some-

[1] Joseph Ratner (ed.), *John Dewey: Philosophy and Social Practice* (New York: G. P. Putnam's Sons, 1963), p. 156 (a reprint of Dewey's article, "Knowledge and Idealization," from *Mind*, July, 1887. pp. 383–396.

how set themselves into proper order without any associational faculty of the mind.

However difficult the material-formal dichotomy might appear, another problem – perhaps philosophy's most persistent curse – the mind-body problem appeared. This problem, accentuated by anatomical and physiological advances of the period, posed the question of how one was to reconcile the abstract and elusive psychological "stuff" (sensations and ideas in their various formulations constituting a mind or soul) with physical "stuff" (actual concrete actions, activities and functions of the living body and its organs, including the brain). Psychology found itself confronted with the task of joining unallied and discrete parts into a continuous and singular whole. By starting with the Cartesian dualism or bifurcation between the mental and the physical, external means in the form of elaborate and complex metaphysical and epistemological assumptions were needed to bring together parts of wholly different natures; but these assumptions turned out to be fruitless. Unanswerable questions arose as to how the mind, or its then nominal counterpart, the soul, could hold sway over the body by keeping in touch with certain parts of the brain.[1] Ultimately, we are left where we started: with a slipshod mixture of discrete parts. Regardless of how inventive a scheme to bring them together might be (as exhibited by Wundtian parallelism and similar such devices of other "apperceptionists") we are still left with the *disjecta membra* forced together into a pseudo-whole.

By the end of the nineteenth century the remarkable discoveries taking place in physiology had put at the disposal of psychology a knowledge of the brain as an immensely complex apparatus of cells, the ends of which could enter into varied relationships with each other as well as with remoter parts of the nervous system.[2] The brain was likewise found to be in the center of a vast sensory-motor system, with sense data being sent from the peripheral sensory nerves to the central nervous system which attends to or interprets the information,

---

[1] L. Edinger, "Brain Anatomy and Psychology," *The Monist*, XI (April, 1901), p. 340.

[2] *Ibid.*, p. 341.

and which, in turn, activates motor nerves initiating a motor response. To be sure, in fact as early as the pre-Socratics, there had been attempts to locate the mind or soul in the brain and to relate it to bodily processes, but psychologists had now succeeded in demonstrating that processes located in physical structures *were* the mind in as much as given units of structure perform specific functions attributable to it (the mind).[1] Psychologists at long last anticipated a real chance to resolve their dilemma once and for all.

With the knowledge that a unit of structure equalled (not paralleled, as Wundt, Münsterburg, Mach and others had contended) a unit of function, as well as with an understanding that all parts – sensory, mental, and motor-muscular – were constituent parts of a singular human action, psychology at last had the means with which to free itself from the mind-body problem. All that psychologists needed to do was to find an appropriate process located in a physical, anatomical structure which performs the functions attributed to the mind in human actions; indeed, this is what they set out to do.

Psychologists postulated that every human act consists first of a peripheral stimulus (or its neural counterpart) standing for sensations, then a central response or attention, standing for the mental idea, and finally the motor response, standing for the action.[2] The bifurcation between the formal and material is alleviated when one considers that the previously conceived constituents of the mind – sensations and the associational faculty or ideas – both have their counterparts localized in a *single* neural process. Similarly, the Cartesian question as to how the mind holds sway over the body by "keeping in touch" with certain parts of the brain is no longer a problem. Taking a unit of anatomical structure as performing a unit of function, the properties of the mind can be located in processes performed primarily by the brain, especially in the

---

[1] John Dewey, *Philosophy and Civilization* (New York: Minton, Balch and Company, 1931), p. 233. (This is the 1896 Reflex Arc Concept paper, only slightly abridged, reproduced in an anthology assembled by Dewey himself, under the title of "The Unit of Behavior," a most suggestive title in terms of broader applications of this theory in his vast and wider ranging works.

[2] John Dewey, "The Reflex Arc Concept in Psychology," *Psychological Review*, III (July, 1896), p. 358.

cerebral cortex, the seat of human intelligence. According to this schema of anatomical localization of function, linkage of the mind with the body is readily discerned, since, by taking the brain to be the structure performing the processes attributable to a mind, both systemic and anatomical connections can be readily ascertained. In the first case, the process that the brain functioning as a mind performs is but part of a total process amounting to an act, the same act involving both the functions of sensations and neuro-muscular action. In the second case, the brain as an anatomical structure is linked to the sensorium by the sensory nerves and also to the muscles by the motor nerves. It can, depending on the portion of the brain involved, voluntarily activate movements through the motor nerves. Both sets of nervous structures are connected to the brain via the afferent and efferent nerves in the spinal column.

While this schema on the whole came nearer to meeting the demand for a general working hypothesis in psychology than any single concept, misconceptions as to the relationship of sensations, thoughts and actions inherent in the nominally displaced older psychology were still in control.[1] To be sure, the physiologists' localization of function theory, holding that a unit of structure performs a unit of function compatible with that said to be performed by the mind in bodily actions, was not at fault. Indeed, this schema became an organizing principle when it passed over into psychology, virtually enabling it to hold together a heretofore unwieldy multiplicity of facts.[2] Psychologists blundered not in methodology or application, but in the manner in which the data was interpreted and systematized. They erred by considering each part of an action – the peripheral stimulus, the central process and the motor response – separately, and then relating them by claiming that they are all involved in a causally reactive chain, or "reflex arc." By doing so, psychologists merely reincarnated the old problem in a new, all too literal, formulation in psychology, one which contained lingering problems

---

[1] *Ibid.*, p. 357.
[2] *Ibid.*

said to be vanquished.[1] The new stimulus-response schema brought with it the rigid distinctions of the older system between sensation, thought, and action which was said to have been overcome.[2] They treated each part of the continuous act as if it were a discrete unit.

The point that Dewey had to make was certainly not a new one. Zeno of Elea, a pre-Socratic philosopher known to us only through secondary sources yet whose paradoxes on motion fevered the brows of both the most obscure and most august thinkers that were to follow him, had this point clearly in hand. He demonstrated that we cannot, regardless of how prolific our source, combine discrete parts and come up with a continuous whole. This, indeed, is Dewey's point: that we cannot say that the whole, meaning the stimulus-response arc, consists *first* of a stimulus, or peripheral sensation, *then* the central response or idea, and *finally* the motor response or action. We have here three discrete parts, complete in themselves yet considered to make up a single behavioristic unit, or reflex arc.[3] This psychological model, namely the one primarily based on James Mark Baldwin's "three elements corresponding to the three elements of the nervous arc," produced the same problems as the earlier philosophers and psychologists had faced, problems that resulted from a disjointed psychological schema.[4] We are again left with what we started: discrete entities complete in themselves and wholly different in nature from their supposed beginning, or with discrete parts involved in a mechanical conjunction of unallied parts.[5] Rather than having a single, continuous process, or *circuit*, we have a step-by-step substitution of presumably reactive parts, or a reflex arc.[6] Since these parts are separate in process, it follows that the functions they represent are similarly separate: the process standing for sensations is separate from that which stands for ideas, the mental phase is separate from that which stands for ideas, and the mental

[1] *Ibid.*, p. 358.
[2] *Ibid.*,
[3] *Ibid.*
[4] *Ibid.*, p. 361.
[5] *Ibid.*, p. 358.
[6] *Ibid.*, p. 360.

phase of the act is similarly detached from the motor-muscular stage. Thus,

(T)he older dualism between sensation and idea is repeated in the current dualism of peripheral and central structures and functions; the older dualism of body and soul finds a distinct echo in the current dualism of stimulus and response.[1]

In order to bring together this rather unwieldy concatenation of material-formal, psychical-physical parts into a single and homogeneous "one," it is necessary to employ one of the same unsound methods which earlier philosopher-psychologists used. One position asserted that the adjustment in the arc had to be effected from outside the unit under study in the form of an extra-experiential "soul," or through the use of the same sort of metaphysical and epistemological surrogates that the Associationalists were forced to employ. The other position asserted, as the followers of David Hartley had done with regard to discrete sensations, that by fortuitously piling up constituent parts in serial order they will somehow "react" into a continuous whole. This adjustment perpetrates the common fallacy of *post hoc, ergo propter hoc,* or the misconception that because one thing comes *after* another, or is adjacent to it, it emerges *because* of that other and is therefore causally or logically related to it and to the entire series of parts in the manner of a simple and elementary push-pull mechanism.[2] But Zeno had shown that we cannot combine discrete parts and come up with a continuous whole; this principle is reiterated by Dewey in his *Reflex Arc* paper.

Dewey was not opposed to the radical new physiological findings or their application to psychological problems in the form of stimulus-response behavior. Rather, he was critical of the manner in which the experimental data was formulated; such faulty organization did not provide a suitable basis for a working hypothesis in psychology.[3] It was the all too literal and absolute nature of the reflex arc concept which drew his

[1] *Ibid.,* p. 357–358.
[2] *Ibid.,* p. 361.
[3] *Ibid.,* p. 358.

censure. In the first incisive formulation of the functionalism suggested by William James, Dewey stated the following:

... the fact is that stimulus and response are not distinctions in existence, but teleological distinctions, that is, distinctions of a functional nature, with reference to reaching or maintaining an end.[1]

Here Dewey expresses the key objection to the concept of the reflex arc in psychology: that the theorists took their respective interpretive schema too literally, as if it were a pre-existent structure to be sought out in the situation under study. By claiming that the S-R phenomenon is made up of the three-staged process, we are required to take an extra-experiential, privileged or almost angelic viewpoint. We as human beings simply do not have the constituent parts merely laid before us to be fitted together in an absolute present, a present beyond the world of flux and continual change. A human action is merely an undifferentiated physical process, an uninterrupted and continuous redistribution of mass in motion, a change in a system of tensions.[2] It is a process just the same as is the falling of a rock, the burning of a log or the movement of the wind.[3] The formal distinctions in this S-R schema are merely interpretive or descriptive modes of understanding used to explain the process at hand. They are neither Baconian facts there to be plucked out of the concrete act, nor Platonic ideas to be sought out in another realm of being.

The nominal S-R designations might well be likened to the relationship of a map to a territory or body of land. The reflex arc configuration which Dewey took to task failed for a very important reason. That is, this map, representing the S-R schema, did not adequately describe the territory, here the process that is the human action. It is not subject to question whether the human act can occur, for it *does* occur, and in order to have done so there must have been a continuous process containing no gaps between constituent neural-muscular components. Since the process is continuous and whole, the functions performed by it, represented by the S-R schema,

---

[1] *Ibid.*, p. 365.
[2] John Dewey, *Philosophy and Civilization*, p. 241.
[3] *Ibid.*

must likewise be formulated so as to be continuous and whole. The process which performs the function of peripheral stimulus is so designated by virtue of its unbroken connection with the central activity or cognitional phase, which, in turn, is defined in terms of its systemic linkage with both the peripheral stimulus and motor response. Even to have these designations at all implies that they must be together in a continuous process.[1] Each constituent gains its nominal designation by virtue of its placement in context with the other participants in the total action.[2] The usual account of the reflex arc configuration thus fails because it breaks the continuity and leaves us with nothing but a series of jerks, the origin of each jerk to be sought outside the unit under consideration.[3]

In developing a philosophical position, we start from where we are; in this case we also start from what we *have*. We start from the perspective of human experience as part of a continual world of flux and change. When we analyze a given human action, the starting point of our inquiry – what we *have* – is not the stimulus, which is gone and temporally past, but a response extant in the present, or, more precisely, a *need* for the response to be consummated in order that the conceptualization of the action be carried out.

While every process in the flux of experience is continuous and unbroken, the discourse or mode of understanding with which we interpret and understand the process is not. It is constantly being broken and contains *ostensible* discontinuities. This is fortunate, for if it were not possible to examine a continuous process over against discontinuities and breaks, we could not reflect on it, come to understand it, and later alter it. In terms of our current discussion of S-R behavior, it is the response which, when it appears, seems to be discontinuous and separate from all that which preceded it; it is an effect with seemingly no cause. The fact that the response appears *ex abrupto* as a novelty seemingly without precedent creates a problem: it must have been caused, actualized or, in the

---

[1] *Ibid.*, p. 240.
[2] *Ibid.*, p. 235.
[3] *Ibid.*, p. 237.

nomenclature of this system, *conditioned* by a stimulus, yet the stimulus is past, and therefore no longer available for examination. In order to discern that what we have at hand is a response, we must determine what conditioned it; we must examine it in the context co-ordinated with its stimulus to call it a response, just as we must determine the cause of an effect before we can call it an effect.[1] Thus, the stimulus must be found and co-ordinated with the apparent break or discontinuity both to constitute a response and cognitively to establish the continuity of action,[2] for by determining that the response is not discontinuous or a break from the behavior that preceded it we have explained *how* it has come about.

The stimulus is always that phase of activity required to be defined in order that the co-ordination be completed ... the search for the stimulus is the search for the exact conditions of actions; that is, for the sake of things which decide how a beginning coordination should be completed.[3]

Since we must search out the beginning of the action in what we *have*, or in available data reconstructed from the past, we must content ourselves with speculation as to what caused or conditioned the tentative response. However, our search which the possible response necessitates is not a haphazard one. Although the sensation which stimulated the response is no longer extant, it metaphorically exists in the sense that the result of its conditioning is evidenced in the present in the form of the response. A sensation cannot be designated a stimulus until it is co-ordinated with its effect, or response, in the context of a single delineated action.[4] Sensation or movement cannot ever be called stimulus or response, respectively, in and of itself.[5] This is not to say that the tentative response is a description of all that led up to it; so to claim is to repeat the psychological or historical fallacy of believing that the structure of an event is "there" to be plucked out of

---

[1] *Ibid.*, p. 245.
[2] John Dewey, "The Reflex Arc Concept in Psychology," 369.
[3] *Ibid.*, p. 368–369.
[4] John Dewey, *Phiolosphy and Civilization*, p. 244.
[5] *Ibid.*

the experience.[1] Rather, the possible response gives the key to the search because we must seek a *particular* sensation that would be capable of causing a *specific* response.[2]

With regard to the flight of an arrow, we cannot simply pile up positions or magnitudes of the arrow and discern the totality of its flight. As Zeno demonstrated, the arrow is only at one position at one time. To investigate its flight, we stop it in thought at a certain position and trace it back to its point of origin, remembering where it was previously and also predicting where it will be if it still is in motion. When we find its point of origin we have a beginning and an end, terminal points between which we might functionally or teleologically, never *literally*, define each idetic or symbolic position (representing a position that is gone) with reference to the part it plays in the arrrow's going from the beginning to the end of the flight. All of this is hypothetical; we start with a continuum and then regress in thought, not in the concrete process which is gone. The same holds true with a human action. We do not start with the experiential beginning of the process, or the stimulus, but with the end, or the possible response; what precedes the stimulus is the whole act.[3] We *start* with a continuum, beginning at the point of completion in experience; this same point is the *beginning* of the reconstruction in discourse of all that came before it. This point, the tentative response, centers the cognitional reconstruction;[4] we indeed start from where we are, which is the point at which the tentative response emerges. We begin with the possible response, with the temporary disintegration of continuity in discourse which necessitates a search for the beginning stimulus to effect a co-ordination. The temporary disintegration which impeded the progress of intelligent conduct by seeming to break the continuity of experience is stopped in thought;[5] all that came before it is set into relief and we seek a proper sensation.[6] When we find it we have what also appears to be a

[1] *Ibid.*, pp. 242–244.
[2] *Ibid.*, pp. 247–247.
[3] *Ibid.*, p. 238.
[4] *Ibid.*, p. 247.
[5] *Ibid.*
[6] *Ibid.*, p. 248.

break from all that preceded it, but when it is co-ordinated with the movement that becomes a response the sensation itself becomes a change in the direction of the process, a beginning of the process – its stimulation[1].

When the proper sensory stimulus is found, continuity is not only established, but the stimulus emerges as the matrix of the action, delineating it and bringing the co-ordination to an issue.[2] By this I mean that with these two terminal points defined, with the stimulus at the experiential beginning or point of nascence and the response at the ending, we have defined a single delineated unit, or 'circuit', that is a human action. Within this background or "matrix" we can define symbolized idetic parts with reference to parts played in reaching or maintaining an end that is the response[3]. Arriving at this stage of inquiry we "cut" the continuum, to borrow a term from Dedekind, but, of course, this "cut" occurs in discourse, not in the continuous flux; we can alter a continuous process, but surely cannot stop it literally or cut it up into neat parcels. The "cut" is analogous to the boundaries on a map; they delimit the territory (here the continuous flux) representationally, never literally. Within this single individuated action we can define constituent parts with reference to bringing about a mutually inclusive end which is the response[4]. All of these factors – sensory, mental and motor-muscular – are all on a par, functionally or teleologically defined with reference to reaching a single inclusive goal. Indeed, we start with a continuum and *then* analytically discern parts, and not vice versa as did those whom Dewey took to task.

In this schema, each member takes on the identity of every other member, all functioning to bring about the same end; the end has gotten thoroughly organized into the means[5]. The sensory stimulus is as much motor-muscular as sensory, for only when it is constituted does the motor-muscular move-

---

[1] *Ibid.*, p. 256.
[2] *Ibid.*, p. 238.
[3] *Ibid.*, p. 242.
[4] *Ibid.*, p. 243.
[5] *Ibid.*, p. 242.

ment become the response. In the same manner, the motor-muscular response is just as much sensory as it is motor-muscular, for only when it is constituted does the sensory element become the stimulus. We do, of course, set these in a serial order, but this ordering or mediation is analytical, in thought or discourse, not literal, in the act proper. These serial-analytical distinctions are made *within* the circuit; they are functional phases of its own mediation,[1] divisions of labor, so to speak. They do not involve separate, self-sufficient parts amalgamated together by the nexus of a presumed reactive *arc*; all are functionally adjusted to each other, but the mechanism and control lies inside, not outside, the act.[2] The response is not separate from the stimulus; it possesses the same original "quale," as Dewey terms it, as the stimulus, but it is merely reinforced or transformed.[3] The designations within the circuit merely explain, in functional or teleological terms, how the *original* quale is so reinforced or transformed.

While the preceding formulation might, upon superficial glance, appear to be a mere reiteration of the older model – that containing the dichotomy or bifurcation – a closer examination of Dewey's criticism should dissuade one from such a notion. The paper under consideration is quite a remarkable one, especially since it was written when the subject fields of philosophy and psychology were not clearly distinguished. Some of the most prominent of psychologists made substantial contributions to philosophy, actually doing philosophy under the guise of psychology. Such psychologists as Baldwin, Münsterberg, Wundt and C. A. Strong, a member of the Columbia psychological department, were leading figures in the field of philosophy. In parallel fashion, James, Dewey, especially during his earlier days, and G. H. Mead, a father of group psychology, revolutionized American psychology, formulating the functional brand, while ostensibly doing philosophy. If the paper under consideration were in keeping with this tradition it would, after having found the S-R formulation inadequate, have propounded an alternative model of a dif-

---

[1] *Ibid.*, p. 248.
[2] *Ibid.*, p. 236.
[3] *Ibid.*

ferent configuration. This, however, did not occur. Remarkably enough, Dewey took the position of contemporary philosophy of science, not entering into psychology, but rather looking over its shoulder and criticizing conceptual formulations, methodology, logic and conclusions.

Dewey accepted the S-R approach, adapting the findings of physiology into a psychological model. However, he found grave fault with the accepted formulation of the findings and their consequent conceptualization. He did not propose an alternate model, but did suggest philosophical modifications within the one already available, suggestions made as a philosopher of the science of psychology. These criticisms within the original framework were: (1) that the constituent parts of sensory stimulus, central attention and motor-muscular response are not separate entities held together by a reflex arc, but are analytical distinctions *within* an unbroken, single delineated whole 'circuit'; (2) these designations in the S-R schema are not formal ones, imposed *ab extra* upon concrete behavior as the older Associationalists imposed formal ideas upon material sense data, but are conceptual symbols or implements of understanding defined with regard to bringing about an end, in this case a response; and (3) we start from the viewpoint of human experience, with what we have, which is not a stimulus, but a possible response.

Dewey's Reflex Arc paper concerned itself with the single stimulus-response activity involved in the action transpiring in the environment of a human being. But human behavior is far more complex than a single S-R action; it involves a multitude of complex and intellectually directed actions. Indeed, it involves the *interaction* of the intelligent organism with its environment or existential matrix. Dewey called this interaction or transaction 'experience'. In this universe of experience, the individual, through a methodology founded on beliefs tested out and validated through action to solve problems, "feels out" his world, thereby both rendering it intelligible and directing the course of the world flux in a constructive way.

The individual's understanding of his relationship to his natural environment does not involve searching for pre-existent knowledge extant "out there" in the material universe; neither does it constitute a contemplative attitude whose purpose is to enjoy self-evident truths to be found in some transcendental realm beyond experience. As it was in the examination of S-R behavior, we start from where we are and we start from what we *have*.

While one aspect of experience is usually emphasized by Deweyan scholars – that of the transaction between the individual and his environment – there is another equally vital component of the experiential process. That aspect is the *continuity* of experience. It was noted on the simpler level of S-R behavior that while continuity of process is not literally broken nor does it contain gaps, it is consistently being symbolically broken in thought. The same holds true on the grander level of human experience. That is, breaks occur in an individual's cognitive understanding of the causative process in the experiential continuum. In the context of Dewey's method of problem solving, at the core of his pragmatic system, this break in the continuity of understanding and the mental disorganization consequent upon it is the emergence of the problem. This is our philosophical starting point; the problem is what we *have* extant in the present.

The main thrust of Dewey's method of problem solving is the resolution of emergent present problems in the future, thereby ameliorating the quality of human experience. However, Dewey does not neglect the past; indeed, he deems the examination of the past the chief decisive phase in thought.[1] This is so because the proximate cause of a problem emerging in the present – that which brought it about – lies not in the present itself, but in the expired past. As the problem, like the possible response, appears *ab abrupto*, the situation which confronts us in the present is indeterminate, since its cause remains yet to be discovered. Judging the nature of the present problem to be the key to inquiry into the probable cause of the problem, we reflect on the elapsed past through the medium of memory, using past experience in solving similar such generalizable problems as our guide. We also use know-

[1] John Dewey, *How We Think* (Boston: D. C. Heath and Company, 1910), p. 118

ledge passed on to us by others as well as by institutions of public education, so that we need not start from scratch, but can be guided by knowledge gained in the past by other individuals.

When we discover the source of a given problem (and such a discovery is always hypothetical, because the past cause is inferred, since it no longer exists) we have re-established continuity between the past and the present which was interrupted. However, this problem solving procedure is far from completed. The problematic situation not only has an edge stretching back to the past, but it also has a forward edge projecting into the future. That is, now that the cause of the problem at hand is known, it must be *resolved* in the future in the consummatory phase of the situation. Just as the possible cause was indeterminate, so now is the choice among possible alternate solutions. The choice as to the course of action appropriate to the solution of the problem is selected on the basis of how other problems of this sort were resolved both publicly and privately. The course of action is the means; the resolution of the problem in the future, on the basis of an understanding of a past cause and a selection of a course of action, is the end.

If the chosen course of action is successful, the problem is resolved, the past cause of the problem is indirectly verified, and the situation is no longer indeterminate. The cause of the problem at one end of the situation and its resolution at the other end define a single delineated unit of experience, or an experience.

Inquiry is the controlled or directed transformation of an indeterminate situation into one that is so determinate in its constituent distinctions and relations as to convert the elements of the original situation into a unified whole.[1]

Just as it was in our examination of rudimentary S-R behavior, we can now delineate constituent components in this unit of experience, rather than trying to fuse together ingredient parts of the process of knowing: thought, action and the material world. All are necessary parts of experience; each is mutually dependent and functionally defined within a single unit of

[1] John Dewey, *Logic: The Theory of Inquiry* (New York: Henry Holt & Co., 1938), pp. 104–105. Dewey's italics omitted.

activity. Again, we *start* with a continuum and *then* abstract constituent parts, and not vice versa. In this way, philosophy is no longer bogged down with the subject-object, mental-physical, ideal-real dilemma as to which is the ontologically prior or ultimately real. Philosophers can instead devote their energies more fruitfully to the solution of more important problems confronting civilization.

Only by analysis and selective abstraction can we differentiate the actual occurrence into two factors, one called organism and the other environment.[1]

As the individual persists in this problem solving activity, he builds up a system of pragmatic universals with which to understand his experiential universe. The attainment of knowledge, then, does not involve seeking out truth either in a realm beyond experience or as Baconian facts "out there" in a material world prior to experience. Once again, we begin *in medias res*: from where we *are* and with what we *have* as intelligent human organisms interacting with an environment of process. Man uses knowledge gained from past experience intelligently to act in the present to bring about desired ends in the future. Writ large to the level of whole societies and cultures, the method, or problem solving, is the mode of human advancement, the *summum bonum* of the philosophy of John Dewey. In virtually every one of the interrelated areas of Dewey's system, whether it be his logic, philosophy of education, ethics or even his esthetics, his method of problem solving remains the core principle: all areas are concerned with means and ends and the solution of problems arising in the experience of human beings.

From the foregoing discussion of Dewey's method of problem solving, a similarity between it and the Hegelian dialectic can be discerned. Solving a problem begins with a breakdown in understanding, a search for the past problem and a plan for amending this problem (thesis), comparing this course of action with alternative ones and arguing its respective merits (antithesis), and finally solving the problem with the consummation of the chosen course of action. If the enacted solution lives up to expectations, it is assimilated by the thinking organism and

[1] John Dewey, *Philosophy and Civilization*, p. 252.

becomes habitual in recurrences of other generalizable problems of this sort (synthesis). This, indeed, is how the intelligent organism comes to understand and to alter its experiential world. But there is one major difference in the schema of Dewey: this process of the attainment of knowledge does not amount to a pre-established and absolute unfolding of a thoroughly determined structure in the direction of an Absolute Ideal or completely perfected reality, one whose determination is beyond man's control. Instead, it is a development of what is essentially Charles Darwin's doctrine of natural selection among the species.[1]

In the theory of Darwin, the constituent members of a given genus or species, through contact, interaction and conflict with each other, other species and environmental hazards, are either able or unable to adapt and either survive or perish. This notion of natural selection consequently implies that concrete, material and participating members of a given species determine variation, structure, plan and form among the organisms under study. This surely is a sort of continuing dialectic in which opposing elements come into conflict and out of which an improved novel element emerges, one better suited for survival; but it is hardly the dialectic of which Hegel wrote. Darwin's process of emergence does not amount to an absolute, pre-established idea; the process of emergence in his system is not harmonious with such factors. Instead, the course of evolution is determined by the interaction of metaphysically indeterminant or free elements. Darwin is concerned with abstracting causal order out of process and not positing it as a pre-existent structure; he is concerned with becoming, rather than being. In short, according to Darwin's formulation, means determine ends and ends define means. From this principle Dewey took his lead: he set the dialectic of Hegel into a Darwinian universe, and thereby substituted the principle of emergence for that of determinism.

Unlike the classical philosophers, who considered life's finite, non-absolute and uncertain nature as an unfortunate short-coming, Dewey considered it germane to a sound prag-

---

[1] John Dewey, *The Influence of Darwin on Philosophy* (New York: Henry Holt & Co., 1190), *passim.*

matic philosophy. In such a situation, man could use the instrumental nature of his mind and action to seek out the source of his problems, solve them and therefore gain knowledge of his own existence and world. Mind and action are complementary and mutually determining elements; mind is not elevated to a high status at the expense of action, as in some traditional systems. Since there are no absolutes, there is always room for growth, improvement and the advancement of knowledge never limited by ultimate, invariant truths.

Dewey saw this instrumentalism as providing man a sense of cosmic importance and a feeling of belonging in the material-biological-social universe in which he evolved and is an integral part. More than this, he is able to embrace the most important feature of the Heraclitean and Parmenidean approaches to philosophy, positions which have been set against each other since they were first conceived. That is, man, an animal organism, is carried along with the flux, which is continuous in its changes, but still may have *relative* permanence, universality, structure and relation, here abstracted from material change and emergence and having no independent reality of their own. In such a formulation, experience, or the interaction of an organism with its environment, is the substitute for the notion of substance in classical philosophy; the pragmatic universals which one generalizes from successful efforts at problem solving supersede the immutable, invariant and transcendental realm of ideas.

To show that Dewey's Reflex Arc paper represented a transitional phase in his philosophy between Hegelianism and pragmatism is not to say that from this point onward he abjured all traditional philosophical principles in favor of those of his own invention. Dewey was too practical to disregard 2,500 years of hard won results of previous philosophical investigation. In particular, many residual features of the fundamental Hegelianism which he rejected continued to be influential in the formulation of his own approach to philosophy as I have pointed out. Dewey was also impressed with Hegel's notion of cultural institutions as representing a socially objective mind upon which individuals are dependent for their mental lives. Hegel was one of the first philosophers to view history contextually and genetically, as a process of development, rather than a telling ot tales, and Dewey was concerned with philosophy as an historical process of development. Most important of all, Dewey embraced the Hegelian primacy of practicality, or the insistence that thought and ideas are not abstruse entities beyond the material world, but we find their locus in man's natural, cultural and historical environment.

In the previous discussion, it was mentioned how Dewey, in his criticism of the reflex arc concept, did not attempt to overthrow the basic formulation, but rather to reconstruct it so as to make it philosophically acceptable. On the larger scale of his pragmatic philosophy, in like fashion he did not desire to tear down and replace philosophical edifices erected by previous philosophers. He wished to *reconstruct* philosophy so as to render it consonant with the nature of his own worldly ambiance, a world not static and stationary, but one exhibiting great advances in the technical, social and intellectual sophistication of mankind. In such a climate of directed change in the order of things, a philosophy presupposing as its primary metaphysical assumptions the static, the stationary and the immutable – one giving minor credence to the efficacy of human action to alter its world – appeared less credible than it once had. Dewey therefore sought to reconstruct previous philosophy so that it would be contextually relevant to a world appearing to its contemporary inhabitants in a markedly different way from the sort of world men of times past confronted and tried to explain in a meaningful way.

The publication of the Reflex Arc paper did far more than represent a watershed between Dewey's Hegelianism and his pragmatism, between absolutism and experimentalism. It marked the beginning of a bold career in philosophy that developed for 50 more years. That mission is best described in terms of the title of one of Dewey's later books: "Reconstruction in Philosophy." From the Reflex Arc paper onward, Dewey undertook the task of reconstructing philosophy so that the locus of its concern, the arena from which it ultimately derives its sustenance and to which it should return the benefits of its wisdom, is the experience of social human beings. The Reflex Arc paper heralded the genesis of this quest.